Perspectives on Participation and Inclusion

Also available from Continuum

Creating an Inclusive School, Mal Leicester
FE Lecturer's Guide to Diversity and Inclusion, Anne-Marie Wright, Jane
  Speare, Susan Colquhoun and Tracey Partridge
Inclusion in Schools, Rosemary Sage
Introduction to Education Studies, Sue Warren
Theory and Practice of Education, David Turner
Widening Participation in Post-Compulsory Education, Liz Thomas

Perspectives on Participation and Inclusion

Engaging Education

Edited by

Suanne Gibson and Joanna Haynes

continuum

Continuum International Publishing Group

The Tower Building   80 Maiden Lane
11 York Road   Suite 704
London SE1 7NX   New York NY 10038

www.continuumbooks.com

British Library Cataloguing-in-Publication Data
A catalogue record for this book is available from the British Library.

ISBN: 978-18470-6020-4 (paperback)
        978-08264-4501-8 (hardcover)

Library of Congress Cataloging-in-Publication Data
A catalog record for this book is available from the Library of Congress.

Typeset by Newgen Imaging Systems Pvt Ltd, Chennai, India
Printed and bound in Great Britain by Athenaeum Press Ltd., Gateshead, Tyne & Wear

Contents

Contributors   ix
Acknowledgements   xi

Introduction   1

PART ONE THE VOICE OF THE LEARNER

1 Inclusion Versus Neo-liberalism: Empowering the 'Other'   11
Suanne Gibson
Inclusion: what, when, why, and
   neo-liberalism – the barrier   12
Starting from the learner's perspective   15
Dialogue and safe spaces versus 'school effectiveness'?   17
Author's note   23

2 Listening to the Voice of the Child in Education   27
Joanna Haynes
Constructs of child as learner   29
So what is child?   31
Children's rights   32
Initiatives to promote children's participation in education   36
Conclusion   40
Author's note   41

PART TWO CRITICAL AND ALTERNATIVE PERSPECTIVES ON
              PARTICIPATION AND INCLUSION

3 Education and After-education: Exploring Learning as a Relational Process   47
Tony Brown
Emotions and learning   48
Secure attachment   51
Conceptions of student   51

The relational psychoanalytic lens   52
Emotion, cognition and student identity   53
Imagination, disturbance and education   55
Identificatory confusion   58
Alternative ways of reading classroom spaces   59
Conclusion   61
Author's note   61

4   **Including Deaf Culture:**
    Deaf Young People and Participation   **64**
    Hannah Smith
    Experiences of exclusion   66
    Inclusion in whose culture?   68
    Specialist provision or inclusion?   70
    Conclusion: learning with and from Deaf Culture   72
    Author's note   73

5   **Freedom, Inclusion and Education**   **76**
    Joanna Haynes
    Interpretations of freedom   77
    Education and political liberation   80
    Experimental and alternative education   81
    Mainstream education: freedom through
        philosophical dialogue   85
    Freedom to think   86
    Conclusion   88
    Author's note   89

6   **Wellbeing and Education**   **91**
    Alan Hutchison
    The idea of wellbeing   92
    What is wellbeing education?   92
    Why wellbeing education now?   93
    Problematizing wellbeing education   98
    Critical voices   98
    Contemporary developments in wellbeing   99
    Conclusion   101
    Author's note   101

7 **Where should Pupils who Experience Social,
Emotional and Behavioural Difficulties (SEBD)
be Educated?** 104
Helen Knowler
Where do I belong? 106
Words matter 107
The historic 'burden' of SEBD 108
Including pupils who experience SEBD 110
Mainstream school or special school:
   does it really matter where pupils are taught? 111
Belonging and school 113
Conclusion 114
Author's note 115

PART THREE **APPROACHES TO PARTICIPATION**

8 **Informal Learning Outdoors** 121
Tony Rea
The nature of informal learning 122
Participation in informal learning outdoors:
   benefits and learner outcomes 125
Current debates about challenge and risk in
   the outdoors and how this might affect participation 126
A pedagogy for outdoor learning? 127
Author's note 131

9 **'E's of Access: e-Learning and Widening
Participation in Education** 134
Steve Wheeler
The Information Age and the knowledge society 135
Digital divides 136
The 'e' is for everything 136
The nature of e-learning 138
Where does the learner fit into the 'e'quation? 139
E is for extended learning 140
E is for enhanced learning 141
E is for everywhere learning 142

E is for exclusion   143
Conclusion   144
Author's note   144

10 Widening Participation in Adult Education   **147**
Roger Cutting
The Parents as Educators Programme   153
Getting going   153
The course design   154
Recruitment   155
Unlocking the door   157
The 'R' word – retention issues   159
The end   160
Evaluating a programme   160
Conclusions   161
Author's note   164

Index   167

Contributors

Tony Brown taught physics in secondary schools before working in primary schools as a mathematics coordinator. In 1982 he began work at University College Cardiff and has remained in higher education. In the last six years he has worked as Head of the Centre for Learning Development at the University of Hull and subsequently as Director of the UK Subject Centre for Education at the University of Bristol. His current research and writing is around the application of psychodynamic theory to explore issues of teaching, learning, curriculum development and student experiences in HE.

Roger Cutting has over fifteen years' experience of teaching in adult education. He developed and managed one of the biggest and most successful Access programmes in the country as well as developing a number of community-based adult education programmes. His background is in environmental science, in which he has numerous publications, but more recently his research interests have turned to environmental education, particularly in relation to adult education.

Suanne Gibson is a Senior Lecturer and Programme Leader for Education Studies at the University of Plymouth. She lectures on the BA Education Studies degree and coordinates the Inclusion and Social Justice Research Network. Suanne has published in the field of Inclusion and is co-author of *Managing Special Educational Needs* (2005, Sage).

Joanna Haynes is a Senior Lecturer in Education Studies at the University of Plymouth. Joanna taught in nursery and primary schools in Glasgow and Bristol and has also worked in teacher education and continuing professional development. She is author of *Children as Philosophers* (2002, 2008 RoutledgeFalmer) and has published in the field of teaching thinking and philosophical enquiry.

Alan Hutchison has taught in secondary and further education and currently is a Lecturer in Education at the University of Plymouth. He has a particular interest in wellbeing and in transformative educational experience. Current research includes a study of the impact of visiting West Africa on the attitudes, values and professional practice of trainee student teachers.

Helen Knowler has been a primary school teacher and a Local Authority Advisory teacher supporting pupils who experience SEBD and currently teaches on the Integrated Masters Programme at the University of Plymouth. Her current interest is upon the training and professional development of those staff who support pupils identified has having SEBD.

Tony Rea is Lecturer in Education at the University of Plymouth. His main research interests are in outdoor learning. He is the author of a number of recent papers (Rea 2007, 2008) and book chapters (Waite and Rea, 2007) in this area of education. In his spare time Tony enjoys sailing and hill walking.

Hannah Smith is Lecturer in Education Studies at the University of Plymouth. She has worked with young Deaf people, taught English Literature at the University of Reading and contributed to family research projects at the think-tank Demos. Her research interests include: inclusive and special education, Deaf Culture and sign language, children's literature and constructions of childhood. She is interested in how society constructs people as different and the subsequent impact this has in educational and social settings.

Steve Wheeler is a Senior Lecturer in ICT and Education at the University of Plymouth and is Coordinator of Education Development and Technology Mediated Learning in the Faculty of Education. He convenes the University e-Learning Research Network, is a Fellow of The European Distance & E-Learning Network (EDEN) and Chair of IFIP Working Group 3.6 on Distance Education. His most recent book, *The Digital Classroom*, was published in 2008 by Routledge.

Acknowledgements

Joanna would like to thank the staff and children at Tuckswood First School, Norwich and Gallions Primary School, Beckton, London, who make visitors so welcome and are committed to working for inclusion.

Suanne would like to thank the residents at Lee Cottage, Lisnaskea, for taking time to meet and chat about their lives, also her colleagues and students who, through dialogue and practice, engage regularly with the ideas in this text. The aforementioned are the inspiration behind much of this work.

Introduction

Perspectives on Participation and Inclusion: Engaging Education is a critical response to significant developments in the field of Education Studies. In particular we attempt to unpack popular policy initiatives, locating their origins, aims and impact upon the wide and varied field of Education. 'Education' as a philosophical and practical endeavour is viewed in a holistic way in our work. We come to our text with the view that 'Education' as ideology and experience is often misunderstood and misapplied in the mainstream context. Education is not merely schooling.

Each author holds a particular philosophical view on 'Education' as theory and practice. Each chapter explores this view, placing it in the context of the author's lived experiences and professional life. Our aim is to provide the reader with a critical platform upon which to explore 'Education' as theory and practice. In explaining and justifying our views and practice vis-à-vis participation and inclusion we refer to a range of educational philosophies and ideas.

Inclusive thinking in Education has become popular in UK and global policy and practice. Advocates of inclusive education predicate their philosophy on arguments of social justice and ideals of the Just and Good society (Ainscow, 1999; Thomas and Loxley, 2001; Allan, 2003; Grayling, 2003). Their aim is that education becomes a transformative and positive experience for all as opposed to an exclusionary process, where commitments to equality and diversity are not just respected ideas but enacted practices. Recent developments in education policy reflect these aims (DfEE, 1998; DfES, 2001, 2003) with emphasis on inclusive education where all, regardless of individual circumstances, preferred learning style or ability can and should be educated together. The need to listen to the views and subjective understandings of all learners regardless of need is asserted (DfES, 2001;

these views are acknowledged as being meaningful, a 'knowledge' worthy of listening to and being acted upon (Cook et al., 2001). We must, however, guard against complacency. Policies on inclusion and participation may exist in government and education circles but this does not automatically result in their translation into practice or the achievement of equity for all learners.

In the following commentary on Freirian philosophy, Noddings provides insight into the necessity of 'empowerment' which, if believing in the significance and importance of each learner including ourselves, needs to be included in our thinking and teaching:

> Oppressed populations need to know something about the forms of oppression and the ways in which the dominant group will try to exploit . . . As they learn . . . oppressed groups also need to generate themes describing their own problems and possible solutions.
>
> (2007: 73)

This political view is relevant to contemporary developments in education as observed in theory, practice and policy and forms the basis for much of our work. We grapple with questions regarding 'purpose of education' and find solace in Brighouse's assertion that, 'the central purpose of education is to promote human flourishing' (2006: 42). That being so, the following pages endeavour to provide accessible ways for the reader to consider what and how to make this happen in aspects of their lives which touch on and contribute to education. This is not a simple process, we therefore call on our readers to engage with difficult questions that may or may not have definite answers. It is through the journey of questioning, investigating through dialogue and through experience that significant educational growth can take place.

What do we mean by equality in education and how do contemporary educationalists work to achieve this? Gibson asserts:

> recent critiques of the sociology of curriculum depict a culture of education which encompasses a particular language, is emergent from a particular set of values, attitudes and experiences all of which stem from the traditions of middle-class nineteenth century England.
>
> (2006: 320)

This may be referred to as the hidden curriculum, where contemporary schooling is founded upon a positivist discourse whose main aim, whether conscious or not, is to transmit the knowledge needed by existing civil society and in so doing reproduce the dominant culture (Giroux cited in Friere, 1985).

The teachings of thinkers such as Giroux and Friere ascribe to the view that there exists a discrepancy in education where policy may assert the agenda of 'pupil participation' and 'inclusive education', yet practice reveals a different reality; that is, 'exclusive education' (Fulcher, 1989; Booth, 2000; Armstrong, 2003a, 2003b). On the surface we may have a view to being inclusive in our schools and universities and providing greater access, yet recent reports (Hallam and Castle, 2001; Milbourne, 2002) suggest a culture of exclusion is still rife in our classrooms, our lecture theatres, our playgrounds and our society.

The depicting of the 'other' as a threat to the status quo with the potential to upset the apple cart of our traditional ways has led to reactionary practices such as middle-class parents buying homes in the catchment areas of the best state schools and school communities, subtly excluding those who may impact negatively on league table results. This reinforces those deemed valid and 'IN' and those deemed 'invalid' and 'OUT'. Exclusion takes different forms: from official school exclusions to more subtle ways (Smyth and Hattam, 2001; Milbourne, 2002). We are suggesting that educationalists who are keen to be an active part of an engaging education first need to familiarize themselves with the philosophies, policies and practices of meaningful pupil participation in education whilst at the same time being critically aware of the reactionary developments and subtle practices that thwart Brighouse's view of education's raison d'être: human flourishing for all (Brighouse, 2006).

The origin of our work is located within significant developments occurring in 'Education' as practice, specifically significant changes and policy developments observed in the educational landscape since the 1980s. We shall be asking the question: how far have we come as a society in realizing the philosophical aims and objectives which worked to inform the foundations of these policies and related practices?

It has been argued that developments in contemporary education policy arise from neo-liberalism (MacConville, 2007) which, in contrast to stated aims, leads to a stultifying of progressive idealism. Once-held notions of critical genius and liberation in the educational practices of critical pedagogues have been surpassed by more simplistic neo-liberal assumptions of educational aims and objectives as witnessed in the practice of and non-critical importance placed on league tables, teacher outputs and performativity. This book builds on Freire's ideas on 'liberating education as engaging education' by suggesting through our work and research ways in which progressive ideas can be resurrected and implemented more fully and meaningfully in our education communities.

Each chapter critically views education as theory and practice and looks below the surface of policies claiming to achieve inclusion and encourage pupil participation. The text will provide guidance drawing on case study examples addressing issues facing education communities today as they attempt to be inclusive, embracing all their learners and practitioners, ensuring full and meaningful participation.

The authors in this collection have all worked in the Faculty of Education at the University of Plymouth. Between them they bring expertise from a wide range of educational settings: formal and informal, special and mainstream, nursery, primary, secondary, further and higher, with children and adults. Over the course of a year, the authors met at intervals to explore the key themes of voice, participation and inclusion and to exchange ideas and experience between and across their professional interests and spheres of practice. This cross-fertilization has been thought-provoking for all of us and helps to inform not only the writing here, but also our future practice as educators actively seeking to widen participation and promote inclusion.

The book is divided into three sections. Part One, Chapters 1 and 2 address the 'Voice of the Learner'; Part Two, Chapters 3 to 7 'Critical and Alternative Perspectives on Participation and Inclusion'; and Part Three, Chapters 8 to 10 'Approaches to Participation'.

In Chapter 1 'Inclusion Versus Neo-liberalism: Empowering the "Other"', Suanne Gibson engages with contemporary developments in the field of inclusive education. In particular she poses the question: How can education practitioners realize the ideals of inclusion as set out in policy documents? Responding to neo-liberal practices in education which in her view have resulted in an overemphasis on teacher efficiency as opposed to learner development, Suanne makes the suggestion that education communities need to create 'safe spaces' for departures from normative practice to be discussed. If space and time is not devoted to accessing, listening to and understanding the voices of that deemed 'other', then development akin to social justice linked with inclusion will remain mere words.

Joanna Haynes, author of Chapter 2 'Listening to the Voice of the Child in Education', asks what we mean when we talk about listening to children in the classroom context and promoting their participation at school. She offers an account of children's rights in the context of discussion about historical and contemporary constructs of child and childhood. She suggests that while there is talk of children being autonomous and independent, practice still operates in too many places with a view of children as limited and inadequate.

Her argument is that practitioners can make a difference in their classrooms. To illustrate this, Joanna includes a case study of one school whose values of inclusion are expressed through well-established initiatives to promote children's voice and participation in the everyday life of the school community.

In Chapter 3 'Education and After-education: Exploring Learning as a Relational Process', Tony Brown poses the question: can education ever be anything other than troublesome? Whether we conceive education in terms of traditional roles of transmission of preferred forms of knowledge, and continuation of revered cultures, or whether we see it as transformative of individuals, the aim of education is always to make different. From a psychoanalytic perspective, becoming *other* whether by choice or prescription, leads inevitably to internal dynamics that challenge the psyche. Psychoanalytic perspectives are relational and to some extent psychodynamic paradigms militate against deficit models of learning teaching. This chapter focuses on the relational in teaching and learning and asks how students and staff manage the transition and transformation that is taken to be education.

Hannah Smith, author of Chapter 4 'Including Deaf Culture: Deaf Young People and Participation', introduces the complex relationship to mainstream hearing cultures experienced by young people who identify themselves as culturally Deaf. Deaf young people experience exclusion on many levels including frequently being taught in a medium which is not their first language, sign language, and consequently missing out on both formal and informal opportunities for learning and social interaction. Policies of inclusion have in some circumstances perpetuated these experiences of exclusion as a result of the closure of many schools for the Deaf. These schools were Deaf communities in which young people found lasting friendships and were enculturated into the language and values of Deaf Culture. Now many Deaf young people are placed in mainstream settings, away from Deaf peers. The task for policy makers and educators is how to ensure that Deaf young people have access to the same high-quality education and have the same life chances as their hearing peers whilst supporting and respecting the right for them to be active members of Deaf communities.

Joanna Haynes' second chapter, Chapter 5 'Freedom, Inclusion and Education', explores her career-long interest in educational approaches that emphasize the development of criticality as a means to address both social inclusion *and* freedom of thought and action. This chapter explores interpretations of freedom and engages with the work of Friere, Illich, Neill and Krishnamurti. Joanna argues that philosophy with children is an empowering pedagogy that promotes children's freedom of expression and participation by strengthening their capacity for dialogue and community building. She illustrates this with children's comments on their experiences of philosophical enquiry in a London primary school.

In Chapter 6 'Wellbeing and Education', Alan Hutchison examines the issue of wellbeing, arguing that an over focus on economic prosperity and widening participation leave crucial questions around human happiness marginalized. This is particularly regrettable at a time when the individualized, competitive and materialistic basis of much contemporary life appears increasingly unable to deliver significant improvements in wellbeing. The chapter makes out a case for an enhanced focus on wellbeing and examines a range of recent related developments inside and outside education as well as highlighting some of the objections raised by critics. In particular, the chapter emphasizes the importance of critically assessing the values informing educational practice and recognizing that inclusion involves a close examination of the cultures and societies in which educational practice takes place.

Helen Knowler, in Chapter 7 'Where should Pupils who Experience Social, Emotional and Behavioural Difficulties (SEBD) be Educated?', explores definitions of participation for pupils who experience Social, Emotional and Behavioural Difficulties, suggesting that the unhelpful binary of inclusion/exclusion has been a major barrier in ensuring that learners described as 'having SEBD' have positive experiences of participation and inclusion. By illuminating barriers to participation Helen argues that the discourses of 'special provision' and 'mainstream provision' as ideologically opposed is not only unhelpful, but that they also places the focus of inclusive practice upon location rather than provision. This chapter challenges the notion that the perceived difficulties of supporting participation and inclusion in this area is always a result of challenging behaviour, but are rather a result of the tensions and conflicts that are sometimes created in schools by policy initiatives that focus upon measurable academic outcomes and the need to 'prove' increased inclusion. Participation, whereby pupils are involved in the decision making that affects them as individuals and have an active involvement in their education, is seen in this chapter as a crucial factor in placing the pupil at the centre, and is the means by which learners can experience meaningful and transformative inclusion in whatever setting they are placed.

Tony Rea, in Chapter 8 'Informal Learning Outdoors', addresses contemporary and significant developments in outdoor education. In particular he critically assesses related education policy and questions the oft-claimed link between outdoor learning and improved academic achievement. He draws on his own research and related empirical studies defining and linking informal education with effective inclusive education.

In Chapter 9 '"E"s of access', Steve Wheeler focuses on the use of e-learning in education, providing critical commentary on how digital technologies can be used to widen participation and provide opportunities of access to disenfranchised learners. There is focus on the digital divide and the potential of technology to exclude as well as include. Steve discusses the social and cultural contexts of education drawing upon recent research into a number of e-learning methods and approaches, including mobile devices and emerging internet features such as the social web. He warns that any implementation of learning technology – whether within or outside of the classroom – needs to be decided on the basis of a number of criteria, including student needs, individual differences and preferences. The conclusion being that, where used sensitively and in response to student needs, e-learning has the potential to provide 'everywhere' learning for all.

Roger Cutting's work in Chapter 10 'Widening Participation in Adult Education' discusses the philosophical aims and origins of adult education in the social movements of the nineteenth century and explores the changing face of adult education today. Ideas on it being a tool for emancipation and social justice seem to have been replaced by an economic imperative. The chapter deals with some of the issues surrounding widening participation for socially excluded adult students in education. It includes a case example of a 'Parents as Educators' project in Norwich. This case highlights some of the current challenges and problems surrounding implementation.

It is hoped that by reading and engaging with the ideas and suggestions provided, this book will aid practitioners and students of Education in their aim to understand and implement 'effective, accessible and meaningful' education for all. We aim to make clear that education policy as it currently stands is not enough. Our book is an exploration of critical and transformative pedagogies which foster participation and inclusion. It draws on case studies which seek to exemplify these principles of participation and voice. It provides the reader with complementary ways forward in thinking and practice which take a stand against our stultifying neo-liberal world order.

References

Ainscow, M. (1999), *Understanding the Development of Inclusive Schools*. London: Falmer Press.

Allan, J. (2003), 'Productive pedagogies and the challenge of inclusion', *British Journal of Special Education*, 30(4), 175–179.

Armstrong, D. (2003a), *Experiences of Special Education. Re-evaluating Policy and Practice through Life Stories*. London: RoutledgeFalmer.

Armstrong, D. (2003b), 'Partnership with pupils: problems and possibilities', *Association for Child Psychology and Psychiatry Occasional Papers*, 20, 39–45.

Booth, T. (2000), 'Inclusion and exclusion policy in England: who controls the agenda?', in F. Armstrong, D. Armstrong and L. Barton (eds), *Inclusive Education: policy, contexts and comparative perspectives*. London: David Fulton Publishers.

Brighouse, H. (2006), *On Education: Thinking in Action*. London and New York: Routledge.

Cook, T., Swain, J. and French, S. (2001), 'Voices form segregated schooling towards an inclusive education system', *Disability and Society*, 16(2), 293–310.

Department for Education and Employment (DfEE) (1998), *Meeting Special Educational Needs: A Programme of Action*. London: HMSO.

Department for Education and Skills (DfES) (2001), *The Code of Practice for Special Educational Needs*. London: HMSO.

DfES (2003), *Every Child Matters: Green Paper*. London: The Stationery Office.

Freire, P. (1985), *The Politics of Education Culture Power and Liberation*. London: Macmillan.

Fulcher, G. (1989), *Disabling Policies: A Comparative Approach to Educational Policy and Disability*. Lewes: Falmer Press.

Gibson, S. (2006), 'Beyond a "culture of silence": inclusive education and the liberation of "voice"', *Disability and Society*, 21(4), 315–329.

Grayling, A.C. (2003), *What is Good*. London: Weidenfeld and Nicholson.

Hallam, S. and Castle, F. (2001), 'Exclusion from school what can prevent it?', *Educational Review*, 53(2), 169–179.

MacConville, R. (ed.), (2007), *Looking at Inclusion*. London: Paul Chapman.

Milbourne, L. (2002), 'Life at the margin: education of young people, social policy and the meaning of social exclusion', *International Journal of Inclusive Education*, 6(4), 325–343.

Noddings, N. (2007), *Philosophy of Education*. Cambridge: Cambridge University Press.

Smyth, J. and Hattam, R. (2001), 'Voiced research as a sociology for understanding "dropping out" of school', *British Journal of Sociology of Education*, 22(3), 401–415.

Thomas, G. and Loxley, A. (2001), *Deconstructing Special Education and Constructing Inclusion*. Buckingham: Open University Press.

Part One
The Voice of the Learner

Inclusion Versus Neo-liberalism: Empowering the 'Other'

Suanne Gibson

Chapter Outline

Inclusion: what, when, why, and neo-liberalism – the barrier   12

Starting from the learner's perspective   15

Dialogue and safe spaces versus 'school effectiveness'?   17

Author's note   23

This chapter defines and evaluates inclusion and related education policies which aim to promote and achieve meaningful and effective education. It critically assesses and evaluates the impact of neo-liberalism as dominant ideology informing government policy and subsequent education practices. It goes beyond a view of effective education as a practice taking place solely within schools. It looks at ways in which meaningful inclusion takes place in a wide range of social contexts.

Drawing on the work of Rosenthal (2001) it is suggested our neo-liberal society promotes sameness, thus valuing the mediocre, promotes one type of knowledge set as linked to and valued by the market place thus subverting difference, perceiving it as a negative rather than potentially innovative challenge to the norm. As Rosenthal suggests:

> to address discrimination and move towards more fully promoting the inclusion agenda, we have to provide regular meaningful dialogues between pupils and teachers, and we have to individually examine and adjust our own less-social perceptions, values and actions. All of us need to experience and hear each other's

points of view and the differences between us have to be acknowledged and explored rather than ignored and denied.

(2001: 385)

My work attempts to provide a way forward for education communities who want to establish and be an active part of a diverse, successful inclusive educational space where all are valued and those deemed 'other' empowered, where difference is embraced and subsequent conflicts, as and when they arise, engaged with and understood in all their richness as opposed to being managed in accordance with technicist approaches. Whilst highlighting that which is holding us back from realizing inclusion, I make suggestions drawing on examples from case study material on how to challenge and turn back the tide of neo-liberalism.

Inclusion: what, when, why, and neo-liberalism – the barrier

Across the UK and arguably the globe, inclusive thinking particularly with regard to the education of children labelled with disability has become widespread. Inclusion is an education philosophy emergent as a departure from integration and related policy. With reference to the UK we can see significant changes taking place partly in response to the 1981 Education Act. Inclusive thinking and the promotion of inclusive education has come into being as part of formative education dialogue, policy and practice (Kenworthy and Whittaker 2000; Mittler 2000; Thomas and Loxley, 2001; Evans and Lunt, 2002; Gibson and Blandford, 2005).

Advocates of inclusive education predicate their philosophy on arguments of social justice and ideals of the Just and Good society (Ainscow, 1999; Allan, 2003). Their aim is that education becomes a transformatory and positive experience for all as opposed to an exclusionary process, where commitments to equality and diversity are not just respected ideals but enacted practices.

Inclusion necessitates the teacher to critically evaluate his/her role as that of facilitator to the mixed ability group and appreciator of all her individual pupils and their achievements. Inclusion is when children and adults are learning together as part of one collective entity. Inclusion is, as Mittler (2000) coins it, a 'Journey', and thus never quite the same for each individual pupil, teacher, school or community. Inclusion celebrates diversity and values all our community members equally regardless of social class, academic ability, gender, ethnicity or sexuality. Inclusion is a school policy, a CPD course, a classroom activity, a local community group initiative. Inclusion can also be a moment; for example, the moment when the learner is engaging effectively and taking what they consider to be a valued role making a valid and worthy contribution to the 'normal' education space.

Recent developments in education policy reflect these aims (DfEE, 1998; DfES, 2001, 2004a, 2004b, 2004c) with emphasis on inclusive education, where all children regardless of need and/or label can and should be educated together. It would appear from reviewing the number and content of government initiatives and policies spearheading inclusion particularly over the last ten years we should be close to realizing these aims in full. Yet research suggests otherwise, noting, for example, the continued exclusion of parents from meaningful dialogue with education professionals regards their children's entitlement, the exclusion of the student voice from significant discussion regards their education – meaning, purpose and impact and the continued poor academic attainment of Black pupils (Cole, 2007; Gunter and Thomson, 2007; Rollock, 2007).

Garner writing in MacConville (2007: x) suggests the reason is because of the language being 'hijacked by politicians, educational opportunists and ideologues', resulting in cynicism at the level of practitioners. I would suggest it goes deeper than this, that the pejorative 'ideology' of 'neo-liberalism' embedded in our government, current education system and society's institutions is causing the face of capital to dictate a limited and 'audited' way forward. The focus as reflected in our current social culture is on the market place, learner as product and economic survival. There is thus a move away from individual social responsibility and the ideals of the collective or community group as highlighted in the post-1960s era (Kenny et al., 2000; Armstrong, 2003; Rose and Shevlin, 2004; Wilson, 2004). Davies coins it well when she states:

> This is a crucial element of the neo-liberal order – the removal of dependence on the social combined with the dream of possessions and wealth for each individual who gets it right . . . the individual is responsible for taking care of him or herself and not dependent on society, such selves . . . no longer have the same responsibility to the social.
>
> (2005: 9)

Responsibility is thus for and to the self, no longer is togetherness and collective responsibility, working as part of a living breathing growing community, paramount. Garner (MacConville, 2007) translates neo-liberalism's impact on inclusion in education with insightful commentary with regard to the 'hijacking' of ideals. He states:

> As evidence of this one has simply to turn to the array of checklists, proformas and indices which seek to assess the extent of inclusion in schools and settings. All emphasise the importance of listening to children yet few offer much evidence that any real listening to children or young people has taken place.
>
> (MacConville, 2007: x)

His words connect with other academics and practitioners attempting to understand barriers to inclusion. Freire's thesis 'Culture of Silence' perceives barriers as inevitable and caused by the current culture and climate in education and society (Freire, 1985). He argues our dominant culture results in the muffling of authentic voices rendering effective, meaningful, that is political, dialogue promoting change in our education communities impossible (Gibson, 2006). Davies, commenting on the impact of neo-liberalism upon education, reflects on its creation and use of oppressive language:

> Oppressive state language – that is currently the language of neo-liberal government is more violent than its bland rather absurd surface would have us believe . . . It is the language in which the auditor is king. It is a language that destroys social responsibility and critique that invites a mindless, consumer-orientated individualism to flourish, and kills off conscience.
>
> (2005: 6)

It is therefore our working within neo-liberal discourses, integral components of our current educational culture, which has hampered our journey towards inclusion. Because of our education system's culture and the hegemony of government policy driving it, we are failing our pupils, particularly in the words of MacConville (2007: 1) those pupils with disabilities who 'actively seek inclusion'.

There is thus a need for change in our mainstream education climate and culture. There is a need to challenge the status quo and whilst working within the prevailing system, to be as inclusive as possible whilst critically aware of the barriers we face. The effect of this may bring about significant change, well stated in the words of Sapon-Shevin (2007: 64), 'By understanding resistance and rejection we can better promote understanding and support.'

Starting from the learner's perspective

Jeremy Harvey cites Lyward's (1970) revelation on the nature and significance of the educator role:

> The thought came to me almost like a blow, these are people – we are all people together in a room – that is the most important fact about this situation. That they were my pupils was a secondary fact completely dwarfed by the first almost alarming realization.
>
> (2006: 21)

Although the above might seem an obvious statement, the significance of the message that each person in a classroom is a valued member, thus of utmost relevance to the learning experiences to be encountered, is profound in our world of tick boxes, targets and speed. Evans and Lunt (2002) note the contradictions between the standards and league tables discourse integral to aspects of neo-liberalism and the inclusive schools discourse. It is because of this, they surmise, that inclusion is hampered.

The words of Lyward, whilst of a different era, speak volumes regarding what the purpose of real and meaningful education should be. To show in one's practice that each member of a group, class or community is a valued member with a relevant and important contribution to make can result in meaningful learning for all. Through the realization that by being together as a collective where each member is valued, a common understanding and sharing of our purpose as a learning thus growing community may be established. Sapon-Shevin in her work challenging simplistic misconstrued notions of inclusion and promoting diverse classrooms as integral to a thriving democracy presents inclusion as a challenge:

> The challenge within inclusive settings is to recognise that every person needs multiple repertoires helping and being helped. Inclusive classrooms can be wonderful places to establish norms and practices that are based on the belief that all people need help, that giving and getting help are good things.
>
> (2007: 42)

Paramount to the effective development of inclusive education spaces is that of empowering the voices of those we work with and for. In relation to this the Code of Practice for Special Educational Needs (DfES, 2001) comments on the importance of pupil participation in the assessment of learning needs, and the compilation and subsequent evaluation of individual education plans. Specifically:

> Children and young people with special educational needs have a unique knowledge of their own needs . . . and views about what sort of help they would like . . . They should, where possible, participate in all the decision-making processes that occur in education including the setting of learning targets and contributing to IEPs.
>
> (DfES, 2001: 27)

There have been many research papers published since the issuing of Code of Practice addressing questions of pupil voice, validity, access and significance. Quicke (2003) writes of the need for 'Reflexivity' in pupil learning, that is, self-reflection on one's learning processes to enable subjective perspectives to be accessed and understood by the learner. Quicke cites (2003: 52): 'We need to know what pupils think they do when they learn (description) but also what they think are the reasons for them learning or not learning (explanatory).' It is suggested that by supporting and enabling reflexive thinking the pupil's needs as understood by the pupil can be accessed and utilized in dialogue with professionals. Hayes (2004) writes of the need for innovation in devising tools to access the pupil's voice in procedures such as the annual review. Her research suggests the use of a 'visual' annual review where pupils with learning difficulty are enabled to take part and make apparent their opinions and views regarding their progress and aspirations. Reflecting these ideas, Mortimer (2004) suggests innovative approaches accessing voice through the use of play with early years children and young children with SEN. This is exemplified in Chapters 2, 4 and 7 where Haynes and colleagues critically explore related developments in inclusive pedagogy.

The above suggestions imply the need for flexible and innovative approaches to dialogue, and furthermore that the responses of the child as emergent from such processes are received and responded to without recourse to their being reinterpreted by the professional. There is, it would seem, a need for empowerment to take place. For the voices of those deemed 'other', those 'failing', those 'excluded', those with 'SEN' to be heard, they and their significant communities need to be empowered. To achieve any real and meaningful inclusive learning experience those with the power to do so need to focus on the empowerment of the traditionally undervalued and excluded, the 'other/s' in our world of white, middle-class, male privilege and achievement. In response to some of the practices proffered, many academics and practitioners suggest that until deeper cultural and structural issues are addressed by local and national education communities, the inclusive aims of their work will remain aims, not meaningful practices (Shevlin et al., 2002; Allan, 2003; Gibson, 2006).

Dialogue and safe spaces versus 'school effectiveness'?

In highlighting what is problematic in our normative practices and education communities, I also suggest what can be done to address and challenge the barrier and negative impact of neo-liberalism. Real innovation and significant steps resulting in effective inclusive education take place when people are freed to think, talk and reflect in a critical environment with support and encouragement from colleagues and relevant others. The politics of the staffroom, target setting of management teams, concern regarding one's career and progression, anxiety arising from impending inspection, are all components of our current education system and they inhibit such practices.

Education communities need to create 'safe spaces' for departures from normative practice to be discussed: space and time devoted to accessing, listening to and understanding the voices and therefore ideas of that deemed 'other'. In so doing positive constructive development of the kind alluded to in the philosophy and related policies of inclusion may take place. Armstrong (2003) suggests the insights revealed in the stories of those previously silenced via medical discourse illuminate the 'hidden' structures of subordination in society, arguably leading to processes of politicization and change (Friere, 1985). Gibson further contends:

> The aims and objectives of inclusive education, policy and research are caught up in political and cultural processes. There is a need to move forward in these aims, to genuinely listen to the voices of those currently being silenced but to do so in a way, which acknowledges the tensions and complexities involved.
>
> (2006: 323)

Lewis (2007), writing about her work in Birmingham listening to the views of young people with learning difficulty, refers to such tensions and complexities but depicts clearly what can be achieved when time and resources are invested, patience and skills utilized and flexible and sensitive approaches developed. She makes the argument that, if serious consideration is given to the processes of hearing diverse views and their challenging nature, subsequent subversion can be prevented.

League tables and the standards discourse are integral components of a neo-liberalist government and society's need to ensure 'knowledge' as capital to invest in our economy rather than knowledge as an enabling force to secure a society where freedom and justice are not mere words but complete and meaningful practices. For those working in the mainstream education context endeavouring to support and empower their pupils and be inclusive, they must first and in a supportive context acknowledge the struggle and tensions involved. Tensions arise due to education communities attempting to be inclusive yet also effective where effectiveness is measured in relation to national league tables and Ofsted reports.

Our mainstream education system operates from the orthodox Received Model of school effectiveness (Gibson and Blandford, 2005) as opposed to a contextual model where the impact of external forces such as local community and environment are acknowledged. As made clear:

> The received model is one which focuses solely on impact of the immediate school environment upon each pupil's learning and development. The received model also identifies effective schools in terms of optimising outcomes for the majority, which is reflected by the perceived importance of government league tables, which merely illustrate a quantifiable approach to outcome and pupil achievement.
>
> (Gibson and Blandford, 2005: 116)

Grace (1998) provides a way in via his alternative vision – a contextual model which he coins a catholic model of school effectiveness. Grace suggests:

> An argument is made that school effectiveness literature and research needs to be more catholic in the sense of being more comprehensive, universal and inclusive in the range of school outcomes, which are taken seriously.
>
> (1998: 120)

By this he means national quality assurance bodies such as Ofsted taking more significant account of qualitative evidence with regards to the effectiveness of a school community as opposed to sole emphasis on quantifiable outcomes such as SAT and GCSE results, that is, that which has more value in a neo-liberal world order. He further elaborates and explains his position by suggesting:

> This could be the beginning . . . of a more democratic, more flexible, more sensitive and more humane practice of school effectiveness research . . . achieved by

extending the important concept of 'value-added' research to include the equally
important concept of 'value-added' inquiry.

(Grace 1998: 121)

The following case studies connect with the critical work of Grace (1998),
Rosenthal (2001) and MacConville (2007). They are narratives written with
reference to the ideas and arguments raised in relation to our problematic
education system, society and related policy.

Case study 1

My first case study is an example of innovation and the struggle for meaningful inclusion within a contextual model of effectiveness (Gibson, 2006). It is a story about the inclusive teaching and learning ideas which emerged when dialogue occurred between and within various levels and groups of a school community. It depicts innate processes of exclusion at various levels of the education system which stand as barrier to innovative ideas being realized. It is an extract taken from an interview with the deputy headteacher of an inner-city secondary school who had been seconded by the LEA because of the school's Ofsted failure. The deputy headteacher is being quoted:

> We were put on Special Measures due to low attainment, poor pupil behaviour, low attendance, poor Special Educational Needs and poor management . . . The kids at our school are very needy kids, they come from a problem area . . . the deputy SENCO working closely with our teachers, LSAs, the parents and their children has set up a family learning programme to have mums involved in teaching their kids, only a half are involved. It is due to a mixture of apathy, low community self-esteem, disorganization, and a hang up that many of the parents have from their own school days.
>
> (Gibson, 2006: 319)

The language used denotes a negative tale, a picture of failure and also of acceptance of the status quo, where it is assumed there are causal links between 'needy kids', 'problem areas', and 'educational failure'. There is also a sense of the positive of a community working together, listening to the voices of parents, pupils and teachers in their attempts to rejuvenate their school community. The language as used by officialdom, in this context Ofsted, and the placing of this school 'under special measures', highlights the location of control and ultimately where power resides. A draconian measure to ensure a deviant school with deviant pupils and deviant teachers located in a deviant community acquiesces and, on failing to do so, deemed a failure and cast aside. For this particular school, closure occurred two years later.

Case study 2

My second case study is a positive tale which highlights the impact of politicization when excluded voices are empowered and subsequent political action takes place. Whilst not of a traditional education context, that is, school community, it none-theless represents an educational community and reflects the significance of what can be achieved when like-minded people come together, seeking empowerment, freedom and justice for the excluded. It also provides insight into where I am coming from, who I am, what I believe in and how my initial perceptions of the 'Other', in this case people with learning disabilities, were challenged and revised.

Much has been written in the field of disability rights, special education and the academic debate regarding models of disability. It is with reference to the field of disability rights that my second story emerges, it is also the story which led to my realization of the level and type of injustice in our so-called developed world and in many ways resulted in my chosen career.

I was twelve and my mum had just become involved as a friend in a local Faith and Light community. The following citation from its website sets out clearly the aims and objectives of Faith and Light (2007):

> Faith and Light is an international community movement bringing together people with a learning disability, their families, carers and friends, particularly young people. It recognizes everyone has their gifts to offer – the ability to welcome others with love and affection and a gift of Celebration. The communities are non-residential and meet together regularly to pray, to share and to celebrate together. The most important thing is to meet and listen to the man, woman or child who is often marginalized in today's society.

My mum was attending one of her first Faith and Light community gatherings and asked me if I would like to come along. I said yes. My first and deep memory of that day was of seeing and being with a group of people, all ages and types, but most importantly of encountering learning and physical disability for the first time. I had a limited understanding of disability, which was by no means a political one. I knew there were in our locality special schools but, as was the case in the mid-1980s, disability was understood as a negative, something to be hidden away and excluded from our 'normal', 'perfect' world. After this initial encounter which led to much confusion, I decided to continue as a friend with Faith and Light, to try to understand and make sense of my confusion whilst at that same time enjoying afternoons spent with new friends, a new and different community yet at the same time a community similar to all others. I have remained a friend with Faith and Light ever since.

Our community would meet twice a month and at these times parents of children and adults with disability would gather to talk about their experiences, achievements, hopes and fears, providing for each other a significant support group and springboard for change. The rest of us would chat, play, sing and generally spend

⇨

time together, the importance here of 'being' together with one another as equals, disability and ability, not seeing difference as a barrier or negative, just a natural part of life to be understood and accepted. The emphasis of Faith and Light is upon the New Testament: the teachings of the Gospel are integral to its rationale and mission statement. It is ecumenical and Christian in outlook and emphasis but accepting and involving people from diverse religious backgrounds. The values of Christianity reflect those of inclusion especially regards valuing each human as a beautiful, significant creation and attempting to understand, accept and learn from that which is 'Other'.

Thus Faith and Light brings people together. It is an international organization and registered charity, and its founding in 1968 and growth worldwide has resulted in many significant departures. One such departure was the devising and building of a care home and independent living centre in my own local town of Lisnaskea, County Fermanagh, Northern Ireland in the 1990s. The need for more effective respite and local residential spaces for families with disability was an issue which emerged from many informal parent chats at our Faith and Light meetings in the late 1980s. From these chats it was decided to hold a public meeting and a committee representing parents, carers and friends in southeast County Fermanagh was established. The committee named itself FACT – Friendship and Caring Trust – and I remember attending many fund-raising initiatives as a teenager during the time of its growth and journey towards the building and establishment of Barnlee, a respite facility, and Lee cottage, an independent living centre for families with disability in County Fermanagh.

I spoke to Barnlee about this chapter and how I hoped to tell the story of Faith and Light and FACT, an example of what can be achieved when inclusive thinking, education, empowerment and political action take place. Thus I would like to thank the trustees of FACT for allowing me to include the following citations: 'FACT: a chronological history' and a citation from Barnlee's recent ten-year anniversary celebrations. The following is an extract from 'FACT – a chronological history' (Gibson, 1997) and tells the story of how a respite centre for families with disability in southeast County Fermanagh was established.

FACT: a chronological history – how it was achieved

June 1990	First public meeting in Castle Park Centre
	The public spoke out about the needs of people with learning disability in the area
	Ten women were commissioned as a steering group
Spring 1991	Starting up grant received from Fermanagh District Council
	Survey carried out within a defined catchment area
	Need established
Autumn 1991	Meetings with statutory bodies
	Partnership with NIH (now known as Oaklee Housing Association)

⇨

January 1992	Second public meeting
	Audience addressed by NIH and Croft Community, Bangor
	Launch of fund-raising campaign
	Launch of family support/area fund-raising groups in Fivemiletown, Lisnaskea, Newtownbutler, Derrylin and Roslea
September 1992	FACT becomes a registered charity
October 1993	Site purchased at Barnhill, Derrylin Road
November 1993	First AGM – £5,641 raised
	Thank you to our community and our fund-raisers
April 1994	Launch of 'Buy-a-Brick' campaign
	Anne-Marie McAleese from the BBC
	Monies confirmed from the DOE
November 1994	First sod turned, T. Chambers & Son, builders on site
December 1994	Second AGM – £9,361 raised
	Thank you to our community and our fund-raisers
April 1995	Stone-laying ceremony with Lady Mayhew
December 1995	Head of home appointed
	Third AGM – £19,144 raised
	Congratulations and thanks to our community and our fund-raisers
February 1996	Building handed over to FACT
March 1996	Open evenings in Barnlee and eight more staff appointed
April 1996	Our first three residents make Barnlee their home
November 1996	FACT (Friendship and Caring Trust) Charitable Association becomes FACT (Friendship and Caring Trust) Ltd Charitable Co.
October 1997	Official opening of Barnlee by Mary, Anne and Bernard

Barnlee has gone from strength to strength since its official opening in 1997. It currently has seventeen residents, thirty staff (including care workers) and five residents in Lee Cottage, which provides independent living for more-able members of the Barnlee community. The following citation summarizes the significance of Barnlee depicting it as the outcome of a political movement where Inclusion was effectively realized once people were empowered:

> In my experience Barnlee and FACT has become a little community of mutual respect, caring friendship and a source of empowering those who are vulnerable to discover their full potential. We have evolved literally from nothing in 1990 to a vibrant caring place reaching out to all in the community who need our help and always struggling to see what else can be done to respond to the needs of the community from which we came.
>
> (Gibson, 2007)

⇨

The most powerful voices are of course those of the residents – the people whose very existence demanded change and through their involvement and empowerment have enabled change in practices and provision for those with disability in this community to be sustained. The richest way to end this chapter is therefore by quoting from these particular thinkers who have had a significant impact on my thinking and the work I do:

I love it here – I have freedom and my own room and have time with my family too.

We have choice about holidays or things to do.

I have freedom to go into town or work if I want.

I enjoy working at the day centre four days a week.

It's our own house.

I love it and I help in the kitchen.

Mary and Sammy are going to the FE college formal (prom) in June.

I can achieve more because of the freedom I have at Barnlee.

(Lee Cottage residents, 2008)

Thanks to the Lee Cottage residents: Sammy Acheson, Ivan George Stewart MacClean, Madge Gilroy, Mary McGovern from Derrylin, Mary Michelle O'Reilly, Ann Rice, Johnny Robinson and Margaret Swift. Their story reflects a Frierian belief in educational experience as political and transformatory and Nodding's (2003) work on the radical impact of cohesive communities. It highlights what can be achieved when people are empowered and work together with the common mission and aim of inclusion. Neo-liberalism whilst presenting itself as a challenge in the journey was ultimately overshadowed by the inclusive aims, objectives and political work of FACT.

Author's note

The experiential learning involved in being a member of a cohesive community such as Faith and Light led to my eyes being opened to the unjust and prejudicial attitudes of many people and organizations towards the less-than-'perfect' in our society. My monthly involvements contribute to my attempts to distance myself from the norms and bias of our Coca Cola, retail-driven, body-beautiful world – attempts which as a human, however, I fail regularly! A related and fundamental development was my own illness and diagnosis with multiple sclerosis, I can now talk openly and make sense of it because of the rich insights and experiences it has given me. It justifies, promotes and secures my need to be a political educationalist.

After a degree in politics as well as involvement in community groups such as Student Community Action in West Belfast in the 1990s, Salesian youth workers in Edinburgh and postgraduate study, somewhere in my subconscious I must have realized 'Education' as discipline and practice was the path to take. It brought me to England where I was fortunate enough to secure a bursary to study for a PhD in the education management of Special Educational Needs, resulting in my current position.

As with most things, it is perhaps when we take time for significant reflection that the parts of the puzzle which is our lives actually come together – that which once seemed to sit uncomfortably with the person we thought we were suddenly fits. I hope that for you, the reader, your puzzle will be as colourful as I consider mine to have so far been and that you will find a calling to practise education as a political and inclusive endeavour and not find yourself succumbing to neo-liberal dictates. We live in a rich, diverse and beautiful world – let us try to retain and express that knowledge in our classrooms, schools and local communities.

Further reading

Armstrong, D. (2003), *Experiences of Special Education. Re-evaluating policy and practice through life stories.* London: RoutledgeFalmer.

Gibson, S. and Blandford, S. (2005), *Managing Special Educational Needs in Mainstream Primary and Secondary Schools.* London: Sage.

Harvey, J. (2006), *Valuing and Educating Young People.* London: Jessica Kingsley.

Noddings, N. (2003), *Happiness and Education.* Cambridge: Cambridge University Press.

References

Ainscow, M. (1999), *Understanding the Development of Inclusive Schools.* London: Falmer Press.

Allan, J. (2003), 'Productive pedagogies and the challenge of inclusion', *British Journal of Special Education*, 30(4), 175–179.

Armstrong, D. (2003), *Experiences of Special Education. Re-evaluating Policy and Practice through Life Stories.* London: RoutledgeFalmer.

Cole, B. (2007), 'Mothers, gender and inclusion in the context of home-school relations', *Support for Learning*, 22(4), 165–173.

Davies, B. (2005), 'The impossibility of intellectual work in neoliberal regimes', *Discourse: Studies in the Cultural Politics of Education*, 26(1), 1–14.

Department for Education and Employment (DfEE) (1998), *Meeting Special Educational Needs: A Programme of Action.* London: HMSO.

Department for Education and Skills (DfES) (2001), *The Code of Practice for Special Educational Needs.* London: HMSO.

DfES (2004a), *Barriers to Inclusion.* London: HMSO.

DfES (2004b), *Every Child Matters: Next Steps.* London: DfES Publications.

DfES (2004c), *Removing Barriers to Achievement: The Government's Strategy for SEN.* London: DfES Publications.

Evans, J. and Lunt, I. (2002), 'Inclusive Education: are there limits?', *European Journal of Special Needs Education*, 17(1), 1–14.

Faith and Light (2007), http://faithandlight.org.uk (accessed 5 January 2008).

Freire, P. (1985), *The Politics of Education. Culture Power and Liberation*. London: Macmillan.

Gibson, A. (1997), *FACT: A Chronological History – How it was Achieved*. FACT: 1 December.

Gibson, A. (2007), 'Inter-church service marks Barnlee memorial garden', *The Fermanagh Herald*, 7 December.

Gibson, S. (2006), 'Beyond a "culture of silence": inclusive education and the liberation of "voice"', *Disability and Society*, 21(4), 315–329.

Gibson, S. and Blandford, S. (2005), *Managing Special Educational Needs in Mainstream Primary and Secondary Schools*. London: Sage.

Grace, G. (1998), 'Realizing the mission: Catholic approaches to school effectiveness', in R. Slee, S. Tomlinson and G. Weiner (eds), *School Effectiveness for Whom? Challenges to the School Effectiveness and School Improvement Movements*. London: Falmer Press.

Grayling, A.C. (2003), *What is Good*. London: Weidenfeld and Nicholson.

Gunter, H. and Thompson, P. (2007), 'Learning about student voice', *Support for Learning*, 22(4), 181–188.

Harvey, J. (2006), *Valuing and Educating Young People*. London: Jessica Kingsley.

Hayes, J. (2004), 'Visual annual reviews: how to include pupils with learning difficulties in their educational reviews', *Support for Learning*, 19(4), 175–180.

Kenny, M., McNeela, E., Shevlin, M. and Daly, T. (2000), *Hidden Voices: Young People with Disability Talk about their Second-level Schooling*. Cork: Bradshaw Books.

Kenworthy, J. and Whittaker, J. (2000), 'Anything to Declare? The struggle for inclusive education and children's rights', *Disability and Society*, 15(2), 219–231.

Lee Cottage residents (2008), Interviews with Suanne Gibson, *Engaging Education: Perspectives on Participation and Inclusion*. Lee Cottage: 31 March.

Lewis, A. (2007), 'Drawing on Experience', *Special*, NASEN, September.

MacConville, R. (ed.), (2007), *Looking at Inclusion*. London: Paul Chapman.

Mittler, P. (2000), *Working Towards Inclusive Education: Social Contexts*. London: David Fulton Publishers.

Mortimer, H. (2004), 'Hearing children's voices in the early years', *Support for Learning*, 19(4), 169–174.

Noddings, N. (2003), *Happiness and Education*. Cambridge: Cambridge University Press.

Quicke, J. (2003), 'Educating the Pupil Voice', *Support for Learning*, 18(2), 51–57.

Rollock, N. (2007), 'Why Black girls don't matter: exploring how race and gender shape academic success in an inner city school', *Support for Learning*, 22(4), 197–202.

Rose, R. and Shevlin, M. (2004), 'Encouraging voices: listening to young people who have been marginalised', *Support for Learning*, 19(4), 155–161.

Rosenthal, H. (2001), 'Discussion paper-working towards inclusion: "I am another other"', *Educational Psychology in Practice*, 17(4), 385–392.

Shapon-Shevin, M. (2007), *Widening the Circle. The Power of Inclusive Classrooms*. Boston, MA: Beacon Press.

Shevlin, M., Kenny, M. and McNeela, E. (2002), 'Curriculum access for pupils with disabilities: an Irish experience', *Disability and Society*, 17(2), 159–169.

Thomas, G. and Loxley, A. (2001), *Deconstructing Special Education and Constructing Inclusion*, Buckingham: Open University Press.

Wilson, L. (2004), 'Towards equality: the voices of young disabled people in Disability Rights Commission Research', *Support for Learning*, 19(4), 162–168.

Listening to the Voice of the Child in Education

Joanna Haynes

2

Chapter Outline

Constructs of child as learner	29
So what is a child?	31
Children's rights	32
Initiatives to promote children's participation in education	36
Conclusion	40
Author's note	41

In the fields of education, childhood and related studies, the past seventy years or so of research and theorizing have increasingly pointed towards the view that children are far more competent than they are usually given credit for by adults. From an early age, children are easily able to participate actively in all aspects of everyday life, when encouraged and included in ways that are sensitive to their growing interests and capacities (Nutbrown, 1996). Today social policy regarding children often refers to the principles and language of human rights, including the rights to participation (UNICEF, 1995). Britain is signatory to the 1989 United Nations Convention on the Rights of the Child and recent policy initiatives such as *Every Child Matters* (DfES, 2003) set out to put such principles into effect across all those public and institutional settings that involve children. Based on the belief that children have historically been disempowered through social and cultural practices that exclude them, this policy is also part of a wider political agenda to promote citizenship and social inclusion among children and young people (www.dfee.gov.tk/cpyu). Those involved professionally with children and young people are developing and engaging with new forms of practice, through consultation with youngsters themselves. These ways of working seek to ensure that children's voices are heard in all matters concerning them.

What exactly do we mean when we talk about listening to children's voices and including children as participants in their learning and schooling? In the first part of this chapter I offer a brief account of some of the different conceptions of the child as learner. The second section considers children's rights. When it comes to their education, how much space is there for children to meaningfully participate within today's schooling? Statements of educational aims often refer to children becoming autonomous and independent learners and having a say in the life of the school. Yet practice has often tended towards a view of childhood as limited and inadequate, focusing on what the child is unable to do yet and on what they will become at some point in the future, rather than on what children already know and can do and their present lived experiences of learning, school, friends, family and community. The third section of the chapter reports on efforts being made in one school to give children more influence in school life. It offers ideas about ways in which adults can work to provide children with a public voice with which to speak their mind. While many of the ideas discussed in this case study are relevant for children of any age, I have deliberately chosen to show what is possible in a first school, in order to counter any argument that participation is not really possible for younger children. Some of the most thoughtful and imaginative ways of including young learners' perspectives seem to be found in provision for the youngest learners. These approaches are relevant for participation and inclusion across all phases of education, for children and adults alike. Other practitioners have much to learn from those who work in the early years.

In this chapter I argue that change in favour of children's freedom of thought and expression and their participation is possible here and now in schools. When children are provided with genuine space to express their ideas, their thinking and talking can help to change the classroom from a place of instruction into a place where education is possible. When students are respected as contributors in the process of meaning making and knowledge creation, schools can be transformed into constructive educational communities. As a practitioner myself, I want to listen to children openly and respectfully, in ways that do not suggest that I already know what they are going to say.

Constructs of child as learner

What are some of the major influences on the ways in which children are seen and heard in the classroom? A brief excursion into the writings of some philosophers reveals a range of different ideas about the child as learner, many of which remain in current usage today. In Ancient Greece, Socratic education involved a form of discipleship, a close relationship designed to create within the student's disposition a desire to discover and use truth to live life. For Plato (427–347 BC), education should focus on an ideal end of knowledge, presented in an ordered, sequential and cumulative curriculum, a process of coming to 'recognize' the truth, a truth that is given. In Plato's Dialogues this ideal is exemplified as a process in which Socrates, as philosophical teacher, uses a distinctive style of questioning to enable the learner to reveal the truth. As we shall see later in the chapter, the idea that education might take the form of questioning and dialogue is one that has once again resurfaced.

Some of the most abiding images of the 'child as learner' in the West are derived from the educational philosophies of Locke (1632–1704) and Rousseau (1712–1778). Locke argued that human knowledge originates in sense perception. At birth he claims, the mind is a clean slate (tabula rasa), on which the data of experience are impressed. Such ideas have resulted in frequent references to the child as a kind of container to be filled with knowledge by the teacher, or, to use today's terms, to have knowledge 'delivered' to them. By contrast, Rousseau believed that the development of human character should follow nature. His account of the child Emile, first published in 1762, emphasizes the idea of readiness as the main key for selecting learning activities through a sequence of developmental stages. He and some of his contemporaries, such as Pestalozzi and Froebel, held that the child's learning should progress from the known to the unknown, from the simple to the complex and the concrete to the abstract. Many practitioners today are still uneasy about the association between young children and abstract concepts, yet from an early age children express very clearly ideas about what's fair or not, what's naughty or not, what's sad or not.

The idea that children need to be ready to learn particular things and that teaching something prematurely might even be harmful to their natural development was a view held by many primary educators in England during the 1960s, influenced by the progressive educational philosophy that had its roots in Rousseau's thinking. Rousseau's idea of letting the child develop naturally resulted in a significant extension in the time period of childhood. For Rousseau, the child was a primitive innocent. For him, childhood constitutes our later self and childhood does not disappear when we become adults. Whilst the efficacy of letting the child develop naturally has been challenged, the view that childhood remains active throughout our lives, influencing us psychologically, emotionally and creatively, is one that gains huge momentum in the twentieth century.

Rousseau's view contrasted very sharply with the dominant one at the time, influenced by John Calvin, who saw childhood as a necessary evil to be passed through as quickly as possible, with minimum time spent on 'child-like' activities such as play. The traditional view showed a good child to be as adult-like as possible. This adult-like or mini-adult construct of child arguably resurfaces in a contemporary culture that positions the child as a consumer of goods and as a service user and this construct can be located in some current discourses of participation.

During the twentieth century, ideas about children's learning drawn from the field of developmental psychology, and supported by empirical work seeking to establish universal accounts of the infant and child to adult maturation process, tended to be in the ascendancy. Such universal accounts of child development, often based on detached observation rather than engaging with children and listening to their ideas, position children as the objects of teaching and research, rather than as subjects with their own stories, interests and views. They tend to position adults as those who always know better what children think or need.

Essentialist perspectives generalize about all children of a certain age and their needs, capacities or primary ways of understanding and they still have a strong hold. These views of children as learners have been challenged in different ways, sometimes by other psychologists challenging earlier empirical findings by redesigning experiments in more child-friendly ways (Donaldson, 1992); by critiques that reveal the politically regulating dimensions of developmental and child-centred discourses of learning (Walkerdine, 1984); by sociological accounts that emphasize the importance of place and culture on children's position and capabilities; and by philosophers and educationalists focusing on the role of experience (Dewey, 1938/1954) or the imagination in teaching and learning (Egan, 1986, 1988; Woods, 1995; Woods and Jeffery, 1996). Some writing about childhood seems to come close to a 'new naturalism', stressing children's capacity to question and explore, to come as 'strangers to the world' and with special imaginative strength (Matthews, 1980, 1994).

These different models of young learners each dispose the teacher to a particular kind of listening.

For Dewey (1859–1952), education begins with experience. Dewey, who was critical of progressive views but in favour of active learning, argued that the belief that all genuine education comes about through experience does not mean that all experiences are genuinely or equally educative and he suggested that some experiences are mis-educative (1938/1954). For Dewey the mediating role of the educator is a critical one in acquainting children with public knowledge. His account of pedagogy attends to process. He sees children as rational, collaborative, active participants in knowledge making, and he sees schools as integral parts of the community, rather than as places of preparation for a future community. These views of children as active thinkers learning through interaction with others are endorsed in the social constructivist psychology associated with Vygotsky and Bruner and in classroom studies emphasizing the significance of classroom talk and children as co-constructors of knowledge (Mercer, 1995).

So what is child?

Friquegnon (1997) suggests that we tend to confuse the terms 'childlike' and 'childish', leading to the conclusion that the desirable intrinsic qualities of childhood must be incompatible with adult responsibility. She argues that human nature and society are not fixed once and for all. Childhood can only be partially defined. Just like other developmental concepts – maturity, youth, adolescence, adulthood, knowledge and progress – the terms 'child' and 'childhood' are value laden and culturally variant. However, basic features of the process to adulthood are not invariant. These are physical and psychological needs, the satisfaction of which enables human potentialities to be realized. Cultures have different views of which qualities and potentialities should be emphasized. The issue of culture is important, particularly when it comes to arguments about a child's freedom of thought and expression, voice and agency.

The question 'What is a child?' focuses on common behavioural indicators of maturation and seems to require an emphasis on establishing similarities between *all* children and differences *between* children and adults. But we could put it another way. The question 'What does it mean to be child?' acknowledges diversity and is more concerned with ways in which childlike qualities inform the range of human experience and understanding. In the branch of philosophy known as phenomenology, it is lived experience that shapes our understanding: our daily lives, what we read, see, hear, touch and feel, through bodily presence. Our bodies also carry the memories of our lived experience, so our childhoods are never completely closed chapters. Bachelard suggests that childhood is 'like a forgotten fire', something that can 'always flare up again within us' (1958/1994). From a psychoanalytic standpoint, Winnicott has written of the connections between what he terms the 'realms of illusion and playfulness' and the realm of creative experience. He suggests that these realms have a vital role in creativity and emphasizes the continuity of 'childlikeness' in human experience (1971/1991). This school of thinking takes the view that 'child' is a dimension of human experience, integral to and simultaneous with its other dimensions: youth, adult, elderly. 'Child' is relational, expressed in interaction with self and others. If it is possible for educators to mobilize their own 'childlikeness', it will shed a different light on listening to the voice/s of other child/ren. We will see how this plays out in practice in the case study on pages 36–40, where recognition of the creative and imaginative qualities of 'child' seems to benefit the whole school community.

Children's rights

So far we have considered some philosophical and psychological influences on the ways in which children are regarded as learners. The human rights movement draws our notice to some important historical, political and legal imperatives for a change in the ways that children are treated at school. The idea that children should enjoy human rights is not new. As early as 1912, Korczac wrote of the child's entitlement to love, respect and the best conditions for growth and development. He asserted the child's right to live in the present, to be him/herself, to be taken seriously, to make mistakes, to have secrets and to enjoy respect for his belongings. He argued for children's entitlement to education as well as the right to resist educational influences which conflict with his/her beliefs. Most striking of all is his inclusion of legal rights such as the right to protest against injustice, to have a Children's Court where he/she can judge and be judged by his peers, and to be defended in a system of justice specialized in childhood (Joseph, 1999: 178–180). This was a radical charter. The Warsaw orphanages Korczac founded before the Second World War operated democratically and the children had their own parliament, court and newspaper, in keeping with Korczac's philosophy.

The 1989 United Nations Convention on the Rights of the Child built on Korczac's ideas. It covers four broad categories including survival rights and developmental rights such as the right to education, play and culture. It makes explicit reference to children's rights to information, freedom of thought, conscience and religion. Protection Rights involve keeping children safe from abuse and exploitation of any kind. Participation Rights make provision for children to take an active part in their communities. These include having a say and the freedom to express views, join groups and to assemble. These rights are to be respected in all areas of children's lives, including their schooling.

As well as laying down Articles for the protection and care of children, the Convention of the Rights of the Child recognizes the child's rights to autonomy, in accordance with her/his stage of development. This implies the goal of maintaining an 'open future' for the child, the awareness of choice and the means to make decisions. The Convention endorses children's rights to express their thoughts, views and feelings and to have these listened to and taken into account in decisions affecting them.

The Declaration of the Rights of the Child states that: 'the child, by reason of his physical and mental immaturity, needs special safeguards and care' (UNICEF, 1995: 3). One of the stickier issues facing adults who seek to respect children's human rights is their reading of, and response to this 'special-ness' and how it is reflected in the maturation process. Some adults prefer the emphasis to be on their responsibilities and duties vis-à-vis children, rather than on the idea of rights for children as such. A further 'special' feature of children's rights is the position of parents and caregivers and the relative weight to be given to their perceptions and wishes by virtue of this role (Archard, 1993). These 'special' features identified as having a bearing on children's rights are not intended to be used by adults as reasons for neglecting the recognition of particular rights, but as a guide to supportive, respectful and inclusive approaches to implementation.

As far as children's competence to express a view is concerned, there has in some quarters been a strong move away from a view of children as somehow unreliable and incapable of exercising choices. Adults working in the education and caring professions in particular are legally required to ensure that children's rights are respected within the framework of acknowledging the competences that are present and developing from earliest infancy. In making appropriate provision to address these rights, adults have to be mindful of children's vulnerability and, at the same time, responsive to their experience and the freshness and originality of perspective that youthfulness can bring. In working with children and seeking to enable their freedom to participate, adults must provide encouragement for the expressiveness of the independent selves of children and support the maintenance of a sense of identity and belonging within a healthy web of relationships in families and communities.

Literature that documents children's advocacy and use of their rights, as well as adults' attempts to respond to these rights, has begun to emerge in the last ten years (Flekkoy and Kaufman, 1997; Holden and Clough, 1998; John, 2003; UNICEF, 1995). Much of this literature focuses on provision and forms of communication that make it not only possible, but also more likely that children will be able to express their views, regardless of age, and on the importance of adults actively removing obstacles to listening to children's voices, including the obstacles in their own hearts and minds (Clark and Moss, 2001; Haynes, 2008; John, 2003; Lancaster and Broadbent, 2003). While there are some inspiring examples of children's participation in this literature, the focus of this advocacy in educational contexts often tends to be concerned with children's participation in the organization and management of administrative, servicing or more peripheral functions of establishments rather than with the *central* business of schools: the content of the curriculum and associated pedagogy. There is generally more talk of 'consultation processes', rather than a drive to re-examine the foundations of all educational interactions and the roles of adults and children within them. School councils have become a popular form for such consultation with varying degrees of success.

Practitioners working in early years are often at the cutting edge of thinking regarding children's participation. The Mosaic approach (Clark and Moss, 2001) is concerned with enabling children to have a voice, from the moment of their birth. Its framework is multi-method, participatory and focused on children's lived experiences. Children might, for example, be offered cameras to use to record and represent their views and when it comes to babies attending a nursery, professionals take special care to engage in regular conversation with parents about what their babies prefer and how things are done at home. Mosiac is founded on the new interest in making room for children's perspectives within the discipline of childhood studies and aims to take listening to children away from reliance on periodic consultation and into everyday ongoing conversation and mutual encounter, where children's participation is integral to all policy development and practice (Clark and Moss, 2001: 10).

The impetus for this major change of orientation to children and young people has come from educational, legal, ethical, economic and social directions. The extension of human rights to children has been a driver, but market forces have also played a part as children and their parents represent considerable purchasing power and can be targeted as consumers. Cultural and social changes in the ways in which children are represented and behave in many aspects of public life have accompanied such economic developments. Particular attention is beginning to be paid to the methods that need to be used in public processes and settings, to ensure that young people, from teenage to the very youngest of children, including babies, have an influence in matters that concern them (Clark and Moss, 2001; Clark et al., 2003; Cousins, 1999).

With these social changes have come conceptual shifts in the ways that children are perceived. As James and Prout (1997) have pointed out, children are no longer seen as 'becomings' but as 'beings' whose thoughts, choices, relationships and concerns are of interest in their own right. Among those who work with children and young people, many adults have begun to reflect on the limitations of their insights into children's lives and a corresponding concern with learning to listen. Reviewing the literature in this emerging field, Clark and colleagues (2003) offer some definitions of listening and participation to reflect these theoretical understandings. Consultation is an element of, but not synonymous with, participation. Participation is more than being periodically consulted about one's views. Participation implies active involvement in decision making and some ownership of the decision-making process; it implies opportunities to question and initiate action. Listening, they suggest, is an active process involving hearing, interpreting and constructing meanings. It is not limited to the spoken word and it is a fundamental stage in the participation process in everyday life (Clark et al., 2003). Clark (2004) argues that listening is central to the learning process, challenging assumptions made by practitioners and raising their expectations of children. She suggests that working with children in a more democratic way can relieve practitioners and parents from the burden of needing to know all the answers and open the space to children's contributions.

In childcare and education settings, the need to pay careful attention to the ways and means of listening to children has come increasingly to the fore (Clark et al., 2003; John, 2003; Clark, 2004). DfES policy (2001) has made it clear that children's participation will make new demands on the listening capacities and skills of educators. The political agenda behind this desire for listening professionals needs to be deconstructed. It can still result in listening in order to monitor or assess thinking, and listening so as to make decisions *for* people. It does not mean that the listening expected of professionals is per se one that is affirming for the learner. Ambivalent messages about professional roles continue to be signalled.

While many countries have adopted the UN charter it is hard to gauge its impact on the lives of children in those countries. To what extent do adults consider Article 12[1] in their professional and personal lives with children? Indeed, are they aware that it exists? According to UNICEF, participation rights allow children to take an active role in their communities and nations. These rights encompass the freedom to express opinions, to have a say in matters affecting their lives, to join associations and to assemble peacefully. The Convention indicates that children should have increased opportunities to participate in the activities of their society and to enjoy appropriate levels of responsibility as they move towards adulthood. Many children carry significant economic or social responsibility in their daily lives. Their vulnerability to exploitation and maltreatment does not have to result in the kind of sheltering that denies them the opportunity to make informed decisions. Education is an area that concerns children deeply.

Initiatives to promote children's participation in education

This section considers the moves made by one small school in Norfolk aiming to listen more effectively to children's voices. These initiatives include the adoption of teaching approaches that make more room for individual expression and build confidence and articulacy, the institution of new consultation structures, relationships and processes that shift patterns of authority, and a responsive, dynamic model of school development. In presenting this case, I suggest that the orientation towards listening to children and enabling their participation is an integral part of putting into practice the inclusive educational values of the school.

A visit to the website of Tuckswood Community First School immediately displays the school's attitude towards its young pupils. Its style is open and informal and the home page and other areas are populated with dozens of children's drawings and photos (http://creative-corner.co.uk/schools/tuckswood/home.html). This small school with just over 100 pupils is situated in an area of Norwich where the social and economic circumstances of families are poor.

The school is by all accounts a welcoming place that sees itself as belonging to the Tuckswood local community.

In the inspection that took place in 2004, the school was reported as excellent in its policy and practice for inclusion (www.ofsted.gov.uk). Such a report is a bonus, but the school community itself is already reflective and constructively self-critical; this is part and parcel of its outlook. The belief in equality of opportunity and inclusiveness is at the heart of everything that goes on in the school. There are a number of features, deeply embedded into practice over time, that constitute this inclusiveness: very good teaching and an innovative curriculum; a supportive ethos and relationships throughout the school; meaningful partnerships with parents and other schools and organizations; a democratic and collaborative style of leadership and organization coupled with an outward looking form of professionalism among the headteacher and all the staff. I was fortunate enough to visit the school in 2004 to try out some new teaching ideas. The members of staff are keenly interested in learning from and taking part in pedagogical research and they have also taken advantage of research trips abroad to inform their teaching and curriculum development. The way that adults working in the school all confidently express their views and openly discuss ideas and listen to one another is mirrored in the way they make a similar space for talking and listening available to their children.

Additional provision to enable the inclusion of children with special educational needs (currently 39 per cent of pupils) from the earliest days of their schooling includes a Nurture Group, as well as a Parent Support Group and family learning initiatives. Critical dimensions of inclusion at Tuckswood are the curriculum itself and the engaging teaching and learning approaches adopted. Through a number of carefully chosen and well-managed innovations, learning has become more enjoyable, more participatory and more accessible and the effectiveness of these innovative approaches is reflected in children's confidence and achievement in many subjects and activities.

Further information

Nurture groups have their origins in the 1970s when they emerged in London to cater for those children who were unable to access the curriculum, either because of late

⇨

development or an inability to regulate their behaviour. The theory of nurture groups stems from the work of Bowlby, and his theories of attachment. Nurture groups are a separate classroom within the school in which children from any class who are having difficulty in the classroom can access the learning in a different form.

In this room children learn through similar experiences to those that many experience at home: cooking, sharing a meal, watching television together. Children who join the nurture group are expected to work in this environment for no longer than four terms, after which they will be integrated back into their classroom on a full-time basis.

They remain part of their class, and are present for registration, assemblies, PE, and end of school with their class. Although a nurture group is a very specific form of learning, the skills and theories behind the group are not exclusive to it. It is a way of learning and an attitude that is carried through all the classes, and relates closely to the values on which the school is based (http://creative-corner.co.uk/schools/tuckswood/WholeChild/index.html).

In the mid-1990s, an approach called philosophy for children[2] was introduced at Tuckswood and the teachers trained in its distinctive method of facilitating questioning and dialogue in a classroom community of enquiry. It has been part and parcel of its curriculum ever since. Philosophy for children values independence of mind, learning through participation and cooperation and democratic decision making. It promotes critical, creative and caring thinking through its distinctive approach to collaborative and reflective dialogue.

One of the influences on its approach to teaching is the Socratic method referred to earlier in this chapter. There are three main aspects of the pedagogy. First, thought-provoking material is presented to the community to open the space for thinking and provoke the search for meaning, including texts, images, objects, music or events. Second, teacher and children work together in a community of enquiry. This is participatory and flexible and creates a safe and respectful setting in which it is possible to take risks in thinking. Participants' questions form the basis of the enquiry. Third, in philosophy for children sessions the teacher facilitates in an open-minded, responsive yet challenging way. She/he is respectful, skilful in listening and questioning in ways that enable participants to express ideas, get greater clarity, explore a wide range of possible answers to questions and to express reasons for their beliefs and theories. The first step is to create a teaching and learning space for enquiry and dialogue. Classroom enquiry has the potential to extend the depth and range of learning experience for all those involved. Chapter 5 in this collection illustrates ways in which philosophy for children at Gallions Primary School in the east end of London stimulates attention to teaching, to facilitation of discussion and to questions of power, freedom and control in relationships among adults and children.

The school's website provides some examples of questions the four- to eight-year-old Tuckswood children have explored through reasoning and dialogue, such as: 'Are animals things?' 'Should we eat animals?' 'How do you know if something is real?' Teachers have built on the success of philosophy sessions through an approach to teaching drama that extends children's questioning, problem solving and creative thinking. These approaches to teaching have proved to be empowering for the children. The 2004 Ofsted report indicates that a key ingredient in the school's success is that children know they are listened to and that their contribution to the development of the school community is valued: The report states:

> The teaching of philosophy has a real impact on learning in all aspects of the curriculum, as children are encouraged to think through ideas and issues, ask relevant questions and justify opinions and beliefs. They use these skills in everything they do.
>
> (www.ofsted.gov.uk)

Since 2000, Tuckswood has also had a school council. The council consists of two representatives from each class, a staff representative and a chairperson. The school council was established to give the children a voice in how the school is organized and an opportunity to make changes in areas they feel do not work. They have a small budget to spend in the way they think is best, but can raise money by schemes of their own. There are committees for the playground, charities, football and the environment and the council has done some serious fund-raising for playground equipment as well as for charities. It has made a huge difference to the amount of representation children have in the running of the school.

Many secondary and primary schools have school councils but few have gone to the same lengths as Tuckswood to ensure that children can participate to the full. In 2002–3, researchers from the University of East Anglia worked with three schools including Tuckswood to investigate ways in which visual means can be used to extend communicative practices amongst children and between children and adults in primary schools in the context of the school councils (Cox et al., 2003). The project team's review of the literature on schools councils indicated that there had been little attention to the processes that take place during school council meetings and, in particular, the level of participation between different groups of children. Working with the researchers, teachers at Tuckswood set out to develop forms of visual communication to increase participation in all aspects of the school council's process. These included ways of sampling pupils' feelings about various elements of the school day, to visual agendas and voting procedures. Tim Taylor, one of the Tuckswood teachers involved in the research project writes:

> In particular it forced us to look very carefully at what we meant by representation and whether what we had in our School Council was real pupil participation in the running of the school or just a talk shop where a small minority of elected representatives where involved but the vast majority of the students where not part of the decision-making process.
>
> (http://creative-corner.co.uk/schools/tuckswood/Philosophy/index.html)

Adults working at Tuckswood know that it is worth listening to children because they have much to contribute and they respect their right to do so. It is one of a number of schools that take children's participation seriously, not because citizenship appeared as a subject in the curriculum, but because they are deeply committed to equality and inclusion.

Conclusion

What stands in the way of full recognition of children's right to have their opinions counted in the education setting? What assumptions, beliefs and anxieties influence communication between adults and children? More often than not where children are concerned, practitioners are still listening *for* rather than listening *to*. Mechanisms and opportunities for children's voices to be heard in the majority of schools remain limited. Many things need to change. Almost certainly this will provoke debate about childhood, about relationships and power, about the nature of knowledge. Children are not citizens-in-waiting, they already belong to communities and can participate in ways that benefit those communities.

While educators do not necessarily enjoy great political influence over educational policy making, adults in schools can choose to become active agents of change. It is possible for all adults to initiate change, just by changing the way they respond when children express their ideas. It is possible for teachers to gradually transform their own classrooms and schools, simply by embarking on some of the kinds of initiatives reported here.

Author's note

In 1990, during a period when I was teaching at a primary school in inner-city Bristol, I watched a series called *The Transformers* on BBC television. One of the programmes featured the work of Matthew Lipman. It was called 'Socrates for Six Year Olds'. What was being said about the philosophical questioning and thinking capacities of young children certainly concurred with my experience, particularly when being with young children outside the school context. I had always been intrigued by young children's questions about the world and how they made me rethink my ideas. My first degree is in philosophy and the prospect of philosophizing with children at school appealed to me as a philosopher and as an educator concerned with social justice and with enabling young learners to build their confidence, voice, powers of expression and reasoning with others. This was just what I was looking for – but how could it be introduced into classrooms in UK schools?

In 1994 I attended a conference on critical thinking in education at the University of East Anglia. Here I met Karin Murris, a Dutch philosopher who had pioneered a way of using Lipman's community of philosophical enquiry using children's picture books. I attended her workshop and that marked the beginning of my involvement with philosophy with children (P4C) and with SAPERE, a charity that promotes P4C (www.sapere.org). I have been involved in the field ever since: philosophizing with children in schools, working with trainees and teachers through initial teacher education and continuing professional development, giving talks and workshops, carrying out research and publishing articles, resources and books about ideas and practice in the field.

Philosophical enquiry is by definition open, critical and reflective and P4C is not a quick fix innovation. It is not something to be done to children. Neither is the approach only relevant to children. Communities of philosophical enquiry exist for all ages and in mixed ages too. I interpret (and aim to practise) philosophy with children as a critical pedagogy that opens up the space for listening and dialogue and an approach that has the potential to make the process of education a transforming one, for teachers and learners alike.

Notes

1. Article 12 states that whenever adults are making a decision that affects a child in any way, the child has the right to give an opinion and to have that opinion taken seriously.
2. Philosophy for children was developed by Professor Matthew Lipman and his associates at the IAPC (Institute for the Advancement of Philosophy for Children) at Montclair State College, New Jersey, USA in the early 1970s and is now practised in more than fifty countries around the world. Philosophy with children (sometimes called P4C) encourages the development of reasonableness, practical wisdom and good judgement by emphasizing the importance of questioning, collaborative enquiry and dialogue (Lipman, 1991, 1993).

References

Archard, D. (1993), *Children: Rights and Childhood*. Abingdon and New York: Routledge.

Bachelard, G. (1958/1994), *The Poetics of Space*. Boston, MA: Beacon Press.

Clark, A. (2004), *Listening as a Way of Life: Why and How We Listen to Young Children*. National Children's Bureau. www.ncb.org.uk/

Clark, A. and Moss, P. (2001), *Listening to Young Children: The Mosaic Approach*. London: National Children's Bureau.

Clark, A., McQuail, S. and Moss, P. (2003), 'Exploring the field of listening to and involving young children', *Research Report 445*. London: DfES.

Cousins, J. (1999), *Listening to Four Year Olds: How they can help us plan their education and care*. London: National Early Years Network.

Cox, A., Robinson-Pant, S., Elliott, B., Jarvis, D., Lawes, S., Millner, E. and Taylor, T. (2003), *Empowering Children through Visual Communication*. University of East Anglia: School of Education and Professional Development. www.uea.ac.uk/

Department for Education and Skills (DfES) (2001), *Learning to Listen: Core Principles for the Involvement of Children and Young People*. DfES: Children and Young People's Unit, Ref. No. CYPUCP1, November, 2001. www.dfee.gov.uk/cypu

DfES (2003), *Every Child Matters: Green Paper*. London: The Stationery Office.

Dewey, J. (1938/1954), *Experience and Education*. New York: The Macmillan Company.

Donaldson, M. (1992), *Human Minds: An Exploration*. London: Penguin.

Egan, K. (1986), *Teaching as Storytelling: An Alternative Approach to Teaching and the Curriculum*. London and Ontario: University of Western Ontario.

Egan, K. (1988), *Primary Understanding: Education in Early Childhood*. London: Routledge.

Flekkoy, M.G. and Kaufman, N.H. (1997), *Rights and Responsibilities in Family and Society*. London and Philadelphia: Jessica Kingsley.

Friquegnon, M.L. (1997), 'What is a Child', *Thinking*, 13(1), 12–16.

Haynes, J. (2008), *Children as Philosophers: Learning through Enquiry and Dialogue in the Primary Classroom*. 2nd edn. London and New York: RoutledgeFalmer.

Holden, C. and Clough, N. (eds), (1998), *Children as Citizens: Education for Participation*. London: Jessica Kingsley.

James, A. and Prout, A. (eds), (1997), *Constructing and Reconstructing Childhood: Contemporary Issues in the Sociological Study of Childhood*. 2nd edn. London and Washington DC: Falmer Press.

John, M. (2003), *Children's Rights and Power: Charging Up for a New Century*. London: Jessica Kingsley.

Joseph, S. (1999), *A Voice for the Child: The Inspirational Words of Janusz Korczac*. London: Thorsons.

Lancaster, P. and Broadbent, V. (2003), *Listening to Young Children*. Buckingham: Open University Press.

Lipman, M. (1991), *Thinking in Education*. Cambridge: Cambridge University Press.

Lipman, M. (ed.), (1993), *Thinking Children and Education*. Dubuque, IA: Kendall/Hunt.

Matthews, G.B. (1980), *Philosophy and the Young Child*. Cambridge, MA: Harvard University Press.

Matthews, G.B. (1994), *The Philosophy of Childhood*. Cambridge, MA and London: Harvard University Press.

Mercer, N. (1995), *The Guided Construction of Knowledge: Talk among Teachers and Learners*. Clevedon: Multilingual Matters.

Nutbrown, C. (ed.), (1996), *Respectful Educators, Capable Learners: Children's Rights and Early Education*. London: Paul Chapman.

United Nations Children's Fund (1995), *The Convention on the Rights of the Child*. London: UK Committee for UNICEF.

Walkerdine, V. (1984), 'Developmental psychology and the child-centred pedagogy', in J. Henriques, J.W. Holloway, C. Unwin, C. Venn and V. Walkerdine (eds), *Changing the Subject: Psychology, Social Regulation and Subjectivity*. London and New York: Routledge.

Winnicott, D.W. (1971/1991), *Playing and Reality*. London: Routledge.

Woods, P. (1995), *Creative Teachers in Primary Schools*. Buckingham: Open University Press.

Woods, P. and Jeffery, B. (1996), *Teachable Moments: The Art of Teaching in Primary Schools*. Buckingham and Philadelphia: Open University Press.

Part Two
Critical and Alternative Perspectives on Participation and Inclusion

Education and After-education: Exploring Learning as a Relational Process

Tony Brown

Chapter Outline

Emotions and learning	48
Secure attachment	51
Conceptions of student	51
The relational psychoanalytic lens	52
Emotion, cognition and student identity	53
Imagination, disturbance and education	55
Identificatory confusion	58
Alternative ways of reading classroom spaces	59
Conclusion	61
Author's note	61

The starting point for this chapter derives from Brown (2005, 2006) on the emotional disturbance associated with student learning. It is further developed here and employs theories of psychodynamics to explore the notion that learning is always a relational activity. The chapter explores learning and teaching from an intrapersonal as well as an interpersonal perspective, using psychodynamically informed interpretations of engagement, participation and inclusion.

The constructivist view argues that brain function is adapted through language, imagery and kinaesthetic learning, to create conceptual models of the world and our experience. What is less obvious in the constructivist model is the role of others in the individual's learning (Bruner, 1973). In his later work, Bruner (1996) addresses shortcomings of individualistic psychology by emphasizing the roles of cultural psychology, narrative and stories, as ways by which we grow to understand the world. However, this emphasis on the interpersonal still leaves the intrapersonal relatively unexplored. Psychoanalytic theory offers an alternative paradigm for studying engagement in education and demands that we see learning differently. Engaging learning has to be interpreted through a study of how we relate to self and others, both in the present and through our past experiences. Effective learning is consequential on 'effective' relating – a notion that needs some exploration.

Emotions and learning

Contemporary discourse often takes the student's desire to learn for granted. Failure to learn, poor grades and drop-out are constructed as part of a discourse of deficit. The student lacks something that needs to be provided or acquired – study skills, confidence or a grasp of English. If the deficit is made up, things can get back to normal. We may be so familiar with these views that it is hard to think in any other way. Surely some students are clever and others aren't? Some have academic writing skills and others lack them? Some need academic support whilst others don't? This kind of thinking is so ingrained it seems obvious, and because it sets up an argument based on polarities, good–bad, able–unable, included–excluded, it limits the range of responses we can make.

A psychoanalytic paradigm asks a fundamentally different question. Because learning is relational, we need to ask what is happening between desire, relating and learning, when disruption occurs? Pimm's (1994) discussion seeks to construct an alternative psychological paradigm for learning and teaching. He recounts the story of a three-year-old girl whose father was killed in a traffic accident. She changed the way she counted (1, 2, 3, . . .) to avoid uttering 'three' which was strongly associated for her with the family triad which had been lost in reality but which she perhaps was seeking to preserve. The knowledge we possess is inseparable from the emotional lives we lead. Disruption can occur in relations with tutors, peers, self and significant others from the past. This produces a shift away from the conclusion that poorly performing students have something wrong with them. It also creates difficult questions to be faced by students, their friends and families and their teachers. Extensive work in France, for example by Nimier (2006) and Weyl-Kailey (1985) draws on hundreds of case studies to examine students' relationships to troublesome knowledge.

If people plagiarize when the rules are fairly clear and the consequences severe, what is it about the student's (or tutor's) relations that give rise to this risky and potentially self-damaging behaviour? Why do we do things to spite ourselves – miss an assignment deadline that we could meet if we tried – 'forget' to attend an important exam or interview? We all commit these self-destructive acts from time to time. This behaviour is often associated with strong emotions, feelings of being discounted, marginalized, unimportant, angry or jealous. They need to be regarded as a significant feature in the learning process.

Strong emotions are very common in education. However, most contemporary paradigms place our emotional responses outside the learning process. Working through a psychoanalytic paradigm requires us to position relations *within* learning rather than *outside*.

> Sasha is at the end of her first year of undergraduate study. Her contribution to sessions has been marred by poor attendance. One piece of assessed coursework is a review of a piece of film music, which she fails to submit. Her next piece is a presentation, to be prepared and circulated to her peers and her tutor one week prior to the event. She fails to supply it on time. She contributes a weak and poorly organized input to the joint presentation. Her tutor requires the written copy and a brief reflective learning log the following week. She fails to submit them. She then claims the tutor 'must have lost' her work. She offers a number of reasons why she no longer has copies of her coursework, or the receipts showing when they were submitted. She is very angry when she finds out she has failed the course and blames her tutor for not warning her about 'the regulations'.

From a psychoanalytic perspective the interesting element in Sasha's story is her anger. It may be directed at herself (perhaps for failing to engage properly with the course, or failing to see herself as good enough for higher education), her peers (perhaps for not giving her the support she needed), or the tutor (perhaps for representing the punishing parent who formally records the fail grade). We cannot know the specific reasons and perhaps even Sasha herself might not know. But we can see that she has failed to relate to her tutor and peers. She may have positioned her tutor as a critical parent, or be jealous of her power or knowledge. She failed to acknowledge that her peers were let down by her poor performance, although as an intelligent person, this may well be 'obvious' to her in terms of rational argument. We can describe her inability to relate in this episode as *failed attachment*, and we can recognize similar behaviour in tutors who fail to respond to students' requests, who cannot keep to deadlines, appointments or contracts with students and colleagues, and who dismiss students and colleagues as second-rate thinkers who lack complexity, or who get angry when their ideas and unreliability are challenged.

> Rashid asks for tutorials on a frequent basis. He regularly hangs around corridors and doorways so that he can question tutors about what he has to do for his coursework assessments. He often has a piece of paper to give them, which he wants them to read and comment on. He tries to arrange to collect these later from the tutor's room. In seminars he sometimes repeats word for word the views of his tutor. For his written exam he writes out entirely from memory, an article previously written by one his tutors.

Rashid's anxiety suggests an excessive dependence on others in authority and over-compliance with (possibly imagined) rules. We can describe his relating as based on an *anxious attachment* that deprives him of the opportunity to form or publicly express his own views. Anxiety and fear rather than anger are the dominant emotions experienced here, and these emotions set into motion behaviours that seriously limit and disrupt learning, with the learner failing to think constructively about developing their own ideas and testing them out.

> Seema failed to attend a final examination. She promised to supply a medical note to show there were extenuating circumstances, but this was never submitted. She was offered a second opportunity to take the exam but turned up a day late having lost her examination slip with the date and time on it. She accused the university of operating in a racist way, making it impossible for her to seek help from staff who were biased against her, and she initiated a formal grievance against the university authorities, which she later withdrew. She went on to repeat the course.

Seema's behaviour indicates a strong self-destructive element. During this difficult period she made no use of the good relationships previously built up with tutors and peers. Instead she went about things entirely on her own. Seema's experience appears to have been an 'us–them' antagonism, focused on the university as a disembodied entity. This can be described as a

destructive detachment, where the object that should be supporting and helping, is attacked in ways that lead to frustration and self-destructive consequences, suggestive of punishment inflicted on the self as a way of attacking
the other.

Secure attachment

Bowlby's attachment theory (Bretherton, 1992) provides valuable insights
into the range of relations that staff and students experience in higher education settings. For the most part, relationships between student and tutor
reflect shared interest, pleasure, mutual recognition and the ability to enjoy
the difference of the other – where the relationship develops as 'being and
being with' rather than 'doing and being done to' (Winnicott, 1971/1991).

Bowlby identifies several distinct tendencies in the formation of attachments – *secure, anxious, ambivalent* and *avoidant*. Secure attachments rest on
a sophisticated sense of self with other, borne out of the successful primary
relation with the principal carer and successful management of anxiety during periods of separation. The growth of independence comes from successful adjustment to separation and fear of loss and the recognition that personal
growth and development is only achieved by overcoming the use of defensive
strategies to protect against anxiety.

The ability to form secure attachments in adolescence and adulthood is
built from the childhood experience of realizing that the mother or principal
carer holds the infant in mind during periods of absence.

For many students, higher education in the UK marks a significant point
of separation from close family and other ties which can resemble earlier sep-
arations and invoke the affective responses associated with them. Students
and tutors who achieved secure attachments in childhood are more likely
to develop and sustain them in adolescence and adulthood. The ability to
form secure attachments is thought essential for effective functioning. The
dramatic expansion of higher education is just one of the changes in the way
it is organized that can make it more difficult for staff and students to form
secure attachments.

Conceptions of student

The economic model of 'student as consumer' has exacerbated problems of
engagement with learning. Students who see education as a purchase are

likely to have lower levels of active engagement with learning than students who see education as transformative.

Consumers (of education) are more likely to focus attention on the products (of learning) while eschewing engagement with the construction of learning. The consumerist contract is to supply a working product – with a money-back guarantee against product failure. In contrast, transformative and growth models of education imply a contract which offers the possibility of change in return for commitment to risk the consequences of deep engagement in the educational experience. Where consumerist approaches to learning prevail, there is a disposition to see education as offering a 'pass' (and quickly) without the need to be touched or emotionally engaged with the learning process. For this reason, the psychoanalytic paradigm is potentially a transformative one: 'potentially' because psychoanalytic theory suggests we have to work through the disturbance that education brings, if we are to benefit from it. The working through is dependent on many things. Fundamentally, it is we the learners who have to commit to working through the mess that education gets us into.

From a psychoanalytic perspective, the consumerist approach to education can only offer a hollow experience. Whilst those who have developed secure attachments are likely to seek meaningful educational experiences and may be able to ignore or resist the consumerist discourse, a consumerist approach poses complex challenges for students (and staff) whose disposition is towards *failed attachment* or *destructive detachment*.

The healthy approach to living is to achieve and sustain *secure attachments* – preferably in infancy, but if not, then in adolescence and adulthood. Education offers opportunities for developing secure attachment, but only as a consequence of deep commitment to change and the associated risks. Education offers new possibilities for those whose attachments are not yet secure, but the perceived risks may be great, and the tendency is to defend against the dangers associated with transformation. A consumerist approach invites a defence against change and thus shores up defences against moving towards more secure attachments.

The relational psychoanalytic lens

Relational psychoanalysis sees the exploration of unconscious phenomena and human development primarily in terms of relating. Both parties are entitled to expect openness, and to explore and question the relationship.

Being ready for change and development demands a permeable psyche, open to the powerful forces of love, desire, envy and hate. Opportunities for transformation come only when one makes oneself vulnerable to these forces, which allow us to see ourselves and others as complex, rounded, flawed human beings.

Engaging education is risky because at its heart is a requirement to study oneself as a relational being. To work through what we know about ourselves and move towards this goal requires commitment to the exploration of our desires and defences: our desire to take the easy route to a 'pass' without being changed by others, and our desire to be punished for being less than good enough. Understanding our desires and defences requires entering the world of Freud's Oedipal relations, love of knowledge, admiration for a tutor, passion for the talents of a creative student. The psychoanalytic lens focuses on love and hate: taboo subjects in these anxious times and more likely explored in literary texts[1] than in education theory and practice.

Engaging education cannot be something done to students by the course, or provided impartially by tutors. It is a messy, lived experience in a two-way street. It demands engagement of all parties, considerable powers of reflection and reflexivity and commitment to open exploration of the power relations between student and tutor. It requires a level of transparency that means putting yourself (whether tutor or student) 'on the line'. Students and tutors can find places to hide from relational challenges. The consequences are missed opportunities for personal growth and insight.

The process of student–tutor relating is a professional one relying on mutuality. It requires recognition of power differences in the tutor–student positions, an openness to share the personal, and an exploration of the ways by which both student and tutor can be advanced by the relational experience.

Emotion, cognition and student identity

Psychological health is an important precursor to engaging in education. Being 'available for learning' requires reflexivity in relation to our emotions and resilience to identity change. Buxton (1981) reported on successful executives in a range of careers who, at considerable personal cost went to great lengths to hide their inability to mathematize. Recent studies of the professional identity of teachers (and student teachers) emphasize the central role of the emotions (Ball and Goodson, 1985; Day, 2004; Day et al., 2006a; Greenhalgh, 1994; Hargreaves, 1998; Nias, 1996; Noddings, 1996; Saltzberger-Wittenberg, 1983), though fewer studies (Coren, 1997) have focused on the emotional context of student learning in higher education. Broader studies that go beyond education and teaching (Damascio, 2000) are beginning to add significantly to the argument that good thinking, good learning, and good decision making are more likely when cognitive and affective processes are fully integrated and fully acknowledged. (In Chapter 7 in this book, Knowler also argues for schools to positively recognize the contribution of the emotions to learning in their responses to pupils who experience SEBD.)

Increasingly the literature challenges the received view that emotion interferes with rational thought and wise decision making. As a neuroscience specialist, Damascio (2000) describes emotion as a crucial component of cognition, arguing that primary emotions are intrinsic states of being – internal processes triggered by events. Secondary emotions are an amalgam of primary emotions and socially learned behaviours. The process of learning how to learn effectively – how to do the right things, *and* how to do things right – requires the integration of primary and socially acquired secondary emotions.

Researchers increasingly describe learning in higher education as much more than knowledge transfer and skill acquisition. As students relinquish direct family influence and begin socializing with more diverse groups, partying and experimenting with drugs (in both legal and illegal forms), taking (or avoiding) responsibility for their own learning, making (or resisting) decisions about vocation, all these contribute to making higher education a considerable challenge. For many it is a constructive and exciting time.

Students entering higher education may well experience some fragmentation of identity during the early period, provoked by questions about *who I am, who I am becoming,* and *who I (don't) want to be(come).* Entry into higher education is likely to challenge the sense of who I am, in complex and often unanticipated ways. Psychological disturbance can occur around the fluctuating integrity of an emergent student self or with the broader sense of identity that a person brings to higher education. Not all disturbance is located initially in the intrapersonal of course. Giroux (2005) reports from the perspective of critical pedagogy on disturbance influenced by neo-liberal policies and their impact on the ideas of studentship. Kelly (1955) developed the theory of personal constructs which exposes shifts over time in the ways that we construct our selves in response to others and to new experiences. (See also the work of the Centre for Personal Construct Psychology, University of Hertfordshire).

Recent work by Day and colleagues (2006a, 2006b) involved a study of teacher and student teacher identities in school settings. Day's research shows that identities in educational settings are neither intrinsically stable nor intrinsically fragmented. Teacher and student identities will sometimes be stable and sometimes be more or less fragmented at different points in time and in different ways. Identities are influenced by a number of life, career and situational factors and are shaped from the interplay between social and cultural forces influencing students and tutors, together with their situated experiences and dimensions such as personal history.

Many students experience strong emotional forces as they engage with their studies. (Roger Cutting illustrates some of these forces in his account of the experiences of adult learners returning to study in Chapter 10.) Unanticipated and strongly felt primary and secondary emotions (Damascio, 2000) emerge in relation both to discipline studies and to relations with peers, tutors and those (e.g., family members and friends) from whom there is now a greater psychological distance. Some strong emotions are associated directly with a shift of loved and hated objects: love or hatred of the discipline being studied (we talk of having a passion for a subject), others with sharing a more intimate learning space with peers and tutors, and with establishing our responses to the space of higher education pedagogy and its boundaries. Sharing a living space and shifts in boundaries relating to privacy and intimacy can be exciting and disturbing.

Imagination, disturbance and education

Education is a potential source of profound disturbance because it can provoke change. Change demands giving up, letting go of old positions. Education threatens the status quo. It offers new opportunities and horizons. We are often ambivalent to our experience of education: we can both desire and fear the change it offers. When the change that education demands is experienced as a challenge to the stability of the psyche, the effects of education may well be resisted, denied or rejected. Identity becomes a contested field accompanied by feelings of excitement at new possibilities, by desires to abandon old positions, by hopes for renewal, by anxieties and resistance to new demands and the expectations of self and other. We may well invest a great many of our desires in education, wishing it to become the transformative vehicle that will turn us into someone new.

In a series of conversations as a mature undergraduate student, Judith expressed a continuing hope for education's power to transform. She sought escape from low-paid work. She wanted to work with people and receive the recognition and respect that professionals deserve. She hoped radiography might provide what she desired, but she found she was required to defer to other health professionals and was phys-ically too removed from patients to develop the type of professional relationships she desired. She did not choose a teacher education course because she wanted to teach, but because it would take her out of low-paid work, give her professional standing and a degree of independence in the workplace. In signing up to education as change, she was unexpectedly overtaken by the break up of her long-term rela-tionship, and by doubts about being found out as someone who had cheated their way into education.

The experience of relating can be particularly disturbing for education students on work placements and student teachers. Students often find them-selves in ambiguous situations where they are neither the designated adult with authority, nor the child/adolescent who must defer to authority. They can find themselves located elsewhere in a transitional space that can be as uncomfortable for some as it is enticing for others.

Teachers in school can also find these situations disturbing, feeling jealous of the freshness of approach that students bring. They may resist relinquishing their power by treating the placement student like a pupil/child. The ambiva-lence affects pupils too: some pupils ignore students or fail to respect them, whilst others fall in love with them and are over familiar, or find they can confide in students more readily than they do their teachers. Some school students resent or fear the absence of their regular teacher. They may feel angry that one adult can deprive them of access to another: perhaps mirroring aspects of their home life. Some student teachers enjoy the idea of the teacher as a source of knowledge but are surprised by the strength of their feelings in relation to the disciplinary role they are expected to adopt. Others find the *not-teacher-and-not-pupil* bubble a seductive and comfortable place to be. They may be reluctant or unable to step outside it into a more adult role and move on in their training when required.

The complex and ambiguous roles they experience in the different spaces that schools provide stand in sharp contrast to the long lists of (behaviourally oriented) 'professional standards' that student teachers are expected to meet, many of which demand mechanistic responses from them in order to assess competence in school. The ambiguity of teacher training reflects a greater ambiguity in contemporary education. For the student teacher, the twin experiences of being (an emergent teacher) and of being required to conform, are a direct consequence of neo-liberalism in education: where those with power espouse a belief in a free-market for education, but at every turn regulate it and thereby claim recognition for (the invented or imagined) positive influences that these changes have brought.

It is not only student teachers who experience identity disturbance. For students on non-vocational courses too, engagement with the education process can be just as challenging. The complex demands, pressures and varying levels of role clarity that accompany university study have an impact on student identity and psychological wellbeing, and create the conditions for what Freud (1916) called an *after-education*, which Britzman describes as stemming from:

> Two dynamic actions [which] allow after-education its diphasic qualities. After-education refers us back to an original flaw made from education: something within its very nature has led it to fail. But it also refers to the work yet to be accomplished, directing us toward new constructions . . . Freud suggests that if education incites pleasure, and if it also attempts to move pleasure closer to reality, then this very trajectory requires that we think about education after the experience of education.
>
> (2003: 4–5)

After-education becomes a possibility when we experience something that carries a strong emotional charge and challenges us here-and-now. Sometimes the emotional charge that accompanies an event is even stronger because we make an unexpected association with an earlier experience that has been held in memory (though perhaps not very accessibly). A student teacher observing a maths lesson, or preparing for their first practical lesson may suddenly recall an experience that they have not thought about for many years. This could be a previous occasion as a child or adolescent when they performed publicly, or where they were assessed in a positive or a negative way. Preparing for work in schools provides considerable opportunity for unexpected associations, which in Britzman's words, relate to a flaw in our earlier education: emotional charge (elation, anger, embarrassment, guilt, pride, fear) of the earlier experience that (often unexpectedly) emerges and is strongly felt again in relation to the current experience. 'What does have a lasting effect? Anything that stimulates, mobilizes, creates feelings belonging to the love–hate spectrum' (Bion, 1991: 362).

After-education can only begin when we work creatively on recent and remembered experiences in ways that lead to new and different constructions where we can see ourselves and possibilities for ourselves and our relating. We are engaged in after-education when we can see ourselves as successful instead of failing, when we transform feelings of paralysing guilt into anger that we can act on, when instead of numbing embarrassment at being a success and the centre of attention, we push ourselves to 'walk the talk'.

Identificatory confusion

One consequence of an after-education is that we may see ourselves in a new light, but not everything we see will please us, or those who know us. We may feel a strong sense of having moved on, of having developed and gained new strength and resolve. On occasions we can be reminded painfully that we have not learned from experience – and we can find ourselves in the same old cycle of behaviour that we hoped we had transcended.

The interaction between our psychic work of building an identity out of new experiences and the unexpected associations with earlier encounters can lead to a loss of resilience or a state of identificatory confusion, putting our identity under threat.

> Students can begin to feel different as soon as they are accepted on a course. For Sally, there was an irreconcilable gap between the maths teacher she had imagined would be possible and the reality of the course. In answer to a question about how she was settling in after one term, she replied:
>
> > I'm still not sure to be perfectly frank with you. A couple of weeks ago I did think, 'Why am I putting us all through this?' To be honest. Because, I thought at my age and at my . . . with my experience, it would be like coming and doing a job of work. And I knew there would be work to do at home, but I didn't think it would be as emotionally draining as my A levels were. But it is.
>
> Sally had a long and successful career in building societies and banks. She was highly motivated, able and keen to succeed with what she saw as her one opportunity
>
> ⇨

to be a student. The greatest disturbance for her was around the guilt she felt about disrupting the family routine and the changes to childcare and housekeeping that becoming a student provoked. Any problem at home, with her husband, with the children and their school, or a backlog of ironing waiting to be done, became associated in Sally's mind with the guilt of her student role, the luxury of having time to study, of indulging her desire to be a teacher.

> I want to be . . . a useful working member of society I suppose. I want a really useful role. It's not having a degree. If . . . if it wasn't vocational I don't think I'd do it because . . . I think it would be too selfish, you know, on the family. I did say to my husband, actually, 'Oh! apparently if you don't get on very well with the teaching side of it, which actually isn't a problem for me at the moment, I feel very comfortable with that side, but if you don't, you can change to a BA.' He said, 'What would be the point of that at your age?' OK his support will only go so far.

Adjusting to life as a student was experienced as a loss of identity rather than a gain. The additional role of student created a sense of confusion and guilt and included a vulnerability to identity change that could not have been predicted during the early stages of application and interview.

Alternative ways of reading classroom spaces

Unexpected associations between our current life and our earliest experiences can draw attention to how we respond to what psychoanalysis calls subject–subject relations, including relating to our self. Our earliest experiences influence how we countenance relationships between teacher and learner at a most fundamental level. The way in which we experience these relations often reflects both our earlier experiences of learning in formal settings and our earliest familial relations.

Formal lectures, seminars and tutorials and informal encounters are all potential spaces for learning and growth. After-education becomes possible when students work through what is returned from the tutor and from peers, though this working through may be done largely at an unconscious level, accessed mostly through associations. Drawing on the work of Winnicott (1971/1991) we can refer to learning spaces as potential or transitional spaces.

The physical attributes are relevant but not paramount. They create a sense of a 'third position' (Ogden, 1999) – an emotional experience rather than a physical arrangement, recognized unconsciously as a space which can be occupied at will for the purposes of observing self, other and self–other relations. The tutor–student power relation means that the tutor plays a significant role in the creation and maintenance of the potential space. The value of the space for student learning hinges in part on the tutor's capacity to take the learner into mind.

> If the patient [learner] does not feel safely taken into the analyst's [tutor's] mind, the observing position of the third is experienced as a barrier to getting in, leading to compliance, hopeless dejection, or hurt anger.
>
> (Benjamin, 2004: 28)

Where the tutor is open to the difference that students bring, the potential space is available for learning to happen. Where the power, knowledge and understanding is transmitted or sensed as available only to the tutor and a privileged few, the potential space becomes sterile and a barrier to learning.

Potential space provides an opportunity for learning *about* but also *beyond* the discipline, where ideas can be developed and challenged, and where students sense they are regarded as legitimate actors in the process of constructing knowledge. What is often reported is that the tutor knows their students in a deep sense and values what they bring.

Part of the process of creating an effective teaching and learning space is that it allows education to be thought of as a vehicle for becoming new, different, un-dreamt-of. According to the group work theories of Bion (1961, 1962), the tutor and students act as container and contained for each other. This is a dynamic that teachers cannot avoid, even though they may resist.

The tutor acting as container has a direct influence on the student's capacity to learn, by containing emerging thoughts, ideas, emotions and fragmentary knowledge. The tutor's incapacity to tolerate the learners' frustration is felt as a disruptive experience by all those involved, whether the educational context is the school, workplace or university.

In constructive learning interactions, the speakers and listeners generate visual and other sensory images that capture the essence, not just of the content of the discussion, but also the whole emotional frame of what is possible and permissible in the student–tutor relation. The student's peers and the tutor can function as *container* and help the student resist a desire for flight into panic, or a denial of intelligence and this helps to avoid the student being 'rescued' by a more articulate other who might step in and take over.

Effective containing allows the continued struggling with prevailing emotions, so that the student can more easily stay with the complexity of their immediate situation. This becomes part of the learning experience rather than being felt as an embarrassment and a barrier to understanding.

> The most crucial decision on which mental growth depends is whether frustration is evaded or faced. Encountering a painful state of mind, does the individual immediately engage in one or more of the numerous defence mechanisms readily available for the purpose of getting rid of the awareness of the frustration.
>
> (Symington and Symington, 1996: 67)

The act of healthy containing returns the content of learning in forms which are sufficiently coherent and tolerable for the learner to work on.

Conclusion

Where does this leave the reader as a learner? The noticing to be done has to be with self and with other, in a relatively detached way at least in part. The main argument of the chapter is that learning is always relational and that we learn more when we work with our personal learning in overlaying the more academic knowledge of the discipline.

Author's note

I began working as a counsellor in the 1980s at the same time as I was developing my ideas around the student teacher's learning experience. My counselling training encouraged me to adopt an approach to research and teaching in which personal narratives became more significant. I continue to find personal stories of learning to be compelling both at an affective level and in challenging theoretical knowledge positions. I have increasingly drawn on psychoanalytic models of learning for synthesizing personal and academic learning in my work with student teachers, post-graduate students and colleagues. The two together make educational sense for me in ways that I can also use for my own learning. The separation of academic and personal by contrast seems increasingly arbitrary and incomplete forms of knowledge.

Note

1. *Educating Rita* by Willy Russell (1983), and *Oleanna* by David Mamet (1992) capture the desire and motivation as well as the resistance, ambiguity and risk that engaging education presents.

References

Ball, S.J. and Goodson, I. (1985), *Teachers' Lives and Careers*. Lewes: Falmer Press.

Benjamin, J. (2004), 'Beyond doer and done to: an intersubjective view of thirdness', *Psychoanalytic Quarterly*, 73, 5–46.

Bion, W. (1961), *Experiences in Groups*. London: Tavistock Publications.

Bion, W. (1962), *Learning From Experience*. London: Heinemann.

Bion, W. (1991), *A Memoir of the Future*. London: Karnac Books.

Bretherton, I. (1992), 'Origins of Attachment Theory: John Bowlby and Mary Ainsworth', *Developmental Psychology*, 28, 759–775.

Britzman, D. (2003), *After-Education: Anna Freud, Melanie Klein and Psychoanalytic Histories of Learning*. Albany: State University of New York Press.

Brown, T. (2005), 'Shifting psychological perspectives on the learning and teaching of mathematics', *For the Learning of Mathematics*, 25, 1 (March). FLM Publishing Association, Edmonton, Alberta, Canada.

Brown, T. (2006), 'Negotiating psychological disturbance in pre-service teacher education courses', *Teaching and Teacher Education*, 22(6), 675–689.

Bruner, J. (1973), *Beyond the Information Given: Studies in the Psychology of Knowing*. Oxford: Norton.

Bruner, J. (1996), *The Culture of Education*. Cambridge, MA: Harvard University Press.

Buxton, L. (1981), *Do you Panic about Maths?: Coping with Maths Anxiety*. London: Heinemann Educational Books.

Coren, A. (1997), *A Psychodynamic Approach to Education*. London: Sheldon Press.

Damascio, A. (2000), *The Feeling of What Happens: Body and Emotion in the Making of Consciousness*. New York: Harcourt Brace.

Day, C. (2004), *A Passion for Teaching*. London: RoutledgeFalmer.

Day, C., Kington, A., Stobart, G. and Sammons, P. (2006a), 'Personal and professional selves of teachers: stable and unstable identities', *British Educational Research Journal*, 32(4), 601–616.

Day, C., Stobart, G., Sammons, P., Kington, A., Gu, Q., Smees, R. and Mujtaba, T. (2006b), *Variations in Teachers' Work, Lives and Effectiveness*. Final Project Report RR743. London: DfES.

Freud, S. (1916), *Introductory Lectures in Psychoanalysis Part III*. SE 16.

Giroux, H. (2005), 'Henry Giroux and the politics of higher education under George W. Bush: an interview', *The Review of Education, Pedagogy, and Cultural Studies*, 27, 95–107.

Greenhalgh, P. (1994), *Emotional Growth and Learning*. London: Routledge.

Hargreaves, A. (1998), 'The emotional practice of teaching', *Teaching and Teacher Education*, 14(8), 835–854.

Kelly, G.A. (1955), *The Psychology of Personal Constructs*. New York: Norton.

Nias, J. (1996), 'Thinking about feeling: the emotions in teaching', *Cambridge Journal of Education*, 26(3), 293–306.

Nimier, J. (2006), *Camille a la haine et . . . Leo adore les maths: l'imaginaire dans l'enseignment*. Lyon: Aleas.

Noddings, N. (1996), 'Stories and affect in teacher education', *Cambridge Journal of Education*, 26(3), 435–447.

Ogden, T.H. (1999), 'The analytic third: an overview', in S. Mitchell and L. Aron (eds), *Relational Psychoanalysis: The Emergence of a Tradition*. Hillsdale, NJ: Analytic Press.

Pimm, D. (1994), 'Another psychology of mathematics education', in P. Ernest (ed.), *Constructing Mathematical Knowledge: Epistemology and Mathematical Education*. London: Falmer Press.

Saltzberger-Wittenberg, I. (1983), *The Emotional Experience of Learning and Teaching*. London: Routledge Kegan Paul.

Symington, J. and Symington, N. (1996), *The Clinical Thinking of Wilfred Bion*. London: Routledge.

Weyl-Kailey, L. (1985), *Victories sur les Maths: Comprendre les cause de l'echec et rehabiliter les nulls en maths*. Paris: Robert Laffont.

Winnicott, D.W. (1971/1991), *Playing and Reality*. London: Routledge.

Including Deaf Culture: Deaf Young People and Participation

Hannah Smith

Chapter Outline

Experiences of exclusion   66
Inclusion in whose culture?   68
Specialist provision or inclusion?   70
Conclusion: learning with and from Deaf Culture   72
Author's note   73

The language we use to describe and categorize people is politically and socially significant. Over the years different terms have emerged which have attempted to label people who we could describe as 'non-hearing'. These terms include: mute, deaf-mute and hearing impaired (Wrigley, 1996: 4). Wrigley argues that the term which is preferred by the non-hearing themselves is 'Deaf' with a capital D (1996: 4). As Oliver Sacks explains, 'Some in the deaf community mark this distinction by a convention whereby audiological deafness is spelled with a small 'd', to distinguish it from Deafness with a big 'd', as a linguistic and cultural entity' (1989: xii). Deafness as a cultural identity is akin then to nationality or racial identity. In this chapter most references will be to those Deaf people who consider themselves to be culturally Deaf. However, references may also be made to wider notions of deafness and 'deaf' people and some sources quoted may use these terms.

Deaf people have in common that their preferred language is a sign language. A distinction is made between the experience of hearing-*loss,* which is considered to be a disability and the ability to Sign, which is an indicator of a cultural identity. There is a tension between these two perspectives which emerge from different world-views – that of the hearing world and the Deaf world. This chapter is interested in how young Deaf people come to negotiate their identities in relation to these world-views through their educational journeys and how, at different points, they may find themselves being labelled as 'disabled' in mainstream culture or as a member of the Deaf community in Deaf culture. These positions come into collision and may cause difficulty, especially when others in power positions have a vested interest in keeping both worlds apart. Young Deaf people might want to have the best of both worlds. They may want to be included in the benefits of mainstream education but to do so via their preferred language, Sign. This chapter explores how such inclusion might be possible.

The emergence of inclusive philosophies of education in the last twenty years has profoundly changed the way that we think about disabled members of society. We now consider equal opportunities in education to be a fundamental human right. However, historically, as we will see in this chapter, Deaf people have experienced exclusion and inequalities when they have been educated in hearing-dominated education systems. Inclusive education can be understood as the policies and practices which aim to end these experiences of exclusion and inequality.

We must question whose values and whose perspectives inform such policies. Does inclusion represent the interests of the Deaf community or does it instead serve the wider goals of mainstream culture? The implication of the word 'to include' suggests a level of assimilation into the mainstream which the members of a minority culture might not want. As with the closure of many schools for the Deaf over the last twenty years, these reforms may be perceived as attacks on Deaf Culture. I use the terms 'inclusion' and 'participation' with some caution. The terms are used here to encompass the right for Deaf people to have access to equality of opportunities in education, although not necessarily through assimilation with mainstream cultures. 'Inclusion' and 'participation' need to be reinterpreted and negotiated with the Deaf community. In order to do this, educators need to engage with critical pedagogies which challenge the structure and curriculum of current educational provision in order to make space for the values and perspectives of Deaf Culture.

In this chapter I refer to 'Deaf young people' although this is a group which in itself encompasses diversities. References are made to Deaf identity and Deaf culture as distinct from mainstream hearing culture. Paddy Ladd introduces the term 'Deafhood' to signify the feeling of belonging that accompanies membership of the Deaf Community: 'Deafhood: This term was developed in

1990 . . . in order to begin the process of defining the existential state of Deaf "being-in-the-world"' (2003: xviii). Sign language is the medium for which this world-view is articulated. Being Deaf is a fluid, changeable phenomenon, like being black, being a woman or being any subject. Some young people may consider their use of sign language and relationships with other Deaf peers as the defining aspects of their identity, whereas others may see this as only a small aspect of an identity that is made up of other significant factors. As Ladd argues: 'Deafhood is not seen as a finite state but as a process by which Deaf individuals come to actualize their Deaf identity, positing that those individuals construct that identity around several differently ordered sets of priorities and principles, which are affected by various factors such as nation, era and class' (2003: xviii).

In this chapter we will explore Deaf young people's experiences of exclusion and their opportunities for inclusion and participation in mainstream hearing society and in the Deaf Community.

Experiences of exclusion

The Conrad Report brought to attention the difficulties experienced by Deaf children in the education system. Conrad's research revealed a picture in which Deaf school leavers were achieving levels well below hearing leavers. Data suggested that the average Deaf school leaver left school with a reading age of nine years (Conrad, 1979). Subsequent research has added to our picture of how and why young Deaf people achieve less well than their hearing peers but as yet no policies have appeared to conclusively tackle the problem. Part of the reason for this is the lack of coordinated research and monitoring of young Deaf people, particularly as more and more individuals are placed in hearing-impaired units in mainstream schools, away from other Deaf peers. Young Deaf people are frequently an overlooked minority, in terms of statistics, research and policy. The lack of data available on the educational achievement of Deaf students in itself reveals something of the exclusion of this group.

However, a number of general trends emerge from the research conducted in the years since the Conrad Report. Deaf learners have been found to 'lag behind hearing learners' and to underachieve in both reading and mathematics (Powers et al., 1998: 1). One study carried out in the US of approximately 6,500 deaf pupils found that the average reading age of 17-year-old Deaf pupils was 9.5 years (Holt, 1993 cited in Powers, 2002a: 3). In the UK context, there have been no major studies since the Conrad Report which have shown an improvement on the average reading age of nine years for Deaf school leavers (Powers, 2002a: 3).

Significantly research has shown no clear correlation between educational achievement and degree of hearing loss (Powers, 1998: 1). It is not then the deaf-ness itself which affects achievement but the way in which young people are disadvantaged by the system. Factors such as the presence of additional dis-abilities, the language used at home and socio-economic background appear to be better indicators of achievement of exam results than degree of hearing loss (ibid.: 1). Type of placement, either special school or mainstream setting, does not appear to be significant when other factors, such as pupil intelligence, are taken into account (ibid.: 1). How effectively Deaf students are helped to access the language of the classroom is significant (ibid.: 3). Young Deaf people may miss out on opportunities for informal learning, knowledge picked up via peers and the media, which is absorbed more easily by hearing young people (ibid.: 3). As Valentine and Skelton argue: 'the limited opportunities that Deaf young people have to understand or communicate with hearing people mean that they often feel very isolated from the world around them, receive limited support and thus a poor start in terms of the acquisition of literacy and lan-guage' (2007: 109). Young Deaf people may be missing out, both inside and outside the classroom, on opportunities to absorb learning. As Liam, a young Deaf man explains:

> Well I do feel there's a kind of inequality cos it's very hard for deaf people to get, to get the opportunities whereas for hearing people it's dead easy they just, they just get all they want, and there's always problems of not understanding what's going on and not getting help. I always feel like I'm lost, like I don't understand what's going on and [hearing] people don't understand.
>
> (cited in Valentine and Skelton, 2007: 109)

As Valentine and Skelton report: 'Hearing teachers and careers officers in mainstream schools (like some hearing families) commonly have very low expectations of Deaf pupils' (2007: 110). They put this down to the poor lan-guage skills that are the result of growing up in hearing families as well as the failings of teachers and careers officers, such as ineffective attempts at communication and 'inappropriate decision-making on behalf of their Deaf young people' (ibid.: 110).

In recent years there has been growing awareness in the social sciences that young people's transitions do not adhere to the traditional 'linear' model (ibid.: 104–5). As Valentine and Skelton argue:

> the traditional transitions model has placed too much emphasis on 'normal' development. Not all young people either aspire to all of these 'norms', or achieve them in a form that can be measured or acknowledged in conventional ways. Rather there is increasing acknowledgment that young people are not a universal category and that their transitions need to be understood within the diverse context of peers, family, communities.
>
> (2007: 105)

There is a connection between the images we share of what is normal, physically, linguistically, and psychologically and the visions the education system constructs of what constitutes a successful young person. Too often it is the individual who is blamed rather than the inflexibility of the system to accommodate them. As Davis argues: 'The "problem" is not the person with disabilities; the problem is the way that normalcy is constructed to create the "problem" of the disabled person' (1997: 24).

A sign language user is a disruption to a firmly established and pervasive societal norm: that speech is the 'natural' way for people to communicate. Derrida challenges this assumption of speech as superior to other forms of communicaton (1974/1998). As Bauman explains: 'Derrida recognises that the voice has no natural primacy over nonphonetic forms of language' (Dirksen and Bauman, 1997: 317). Sign language can be seen as an opportunity to challenge fundamental assumptions about knowledge, language and interaction and to open up alternative pathways and welcome other sources of knowledge. Bauman argues: 'Deafness [. . .] occupies a consummate moment in the deconstruction of Western ontology' (1997: 317). For educational institutions to embrace this 'moment' will require fundamental and difficult changes to occur.

Inclusion in whose culture?

In recent years policy has focused on how to 'include' previously excluded groups into the mainstream. This has been a success for many young people, whose educational opportunities and life chances were being severely limited by the institutionalization they experienced in residential special schools. The closure of many residential schools for the Deaf, however, has been greeted with ambivalence. Deaf schools were historically sites for young Deaf people to meet, socialize and learn sign language and were therefore seen as the bastions of Deaf Culture. It is for this reason that inclusion has been opposed by some in the Deaf community. Ladd cites the translation of the term 'mainstreaming' as the combination of 'two BSL signs to visually represent the suppression of the individual Deaf child by a more powerful overarching system' (2003: xx) to illustrate this belief. When placed in mainstream settings, a young Deaf person may be *included* in the mainstream community and hearing families, but *excluded* from Deaf peers, sign language and their extended family of the Deaf Community. Inclusion may be accompanied by the loss of opportunities for language transmission and socialization into Deaf Culture. The relationship to the majority hearing culture needs to be negotiated, not imposed. As members of a linguistic minority, the Deaf community requires respect from the mainstream in addition to the opportunity to socialize new members. Young Deaf people may draw strength from Deaf peers as well as friendship and opportunities for informal learning. One young Deaf girl, Janice, comments 'you have that kind of bond with people, you mix with Deaf people, you have the same sign language, you feel like you're inside the Deaf world, whereas when you're in the hearing world you don't have the communication, you've got written language, but it's a real relief you can feel really relaxed talking with Deaf people' (Valentine and Skelton, 2007: 115).

For young Deaf people we must think both of how to make relationships with hearing people and the hearing world more positive and of how to facilitate relationships with Deaf peers and with sign language. Deaf young people are bilingual and bicultural (sometimes tri-cultural) and should be supported in the advantages and challenges that this brings them. Like members of other ethnic minority groups, negotiating identity and feelings of belonging to multiple cultural groups may result in tensions and sacrifices. Deaf young people deserve to have the 'best of both worlds', in terms of education, career, relationships and self-esteem. Often, however, they may find themselves unintentionally excluded from educational opportunities or prevented from meeting Deaf peers. In this less than ideal world, with a less than ideal education system, how can we negotiate these twin concerns? A key concern is whether the needs of Deaf young people are best met in specialized or supported mainstream settings.

Powers (2002b) argues that it is possible to work towards 'inclusion' in the context of Deaf education. He offers a notion of 'inclusion' that does not necessarily correspond with mainstream placement: 'inclusion is not a *state* to aim for (e.g., the state where all children are in local mainstream schools) but is more concerned with processes and culture' (2002b: 237). In this conceptualization of inclusion, other meaningful criteria such as 'the maximizing of opportunity, independence, achievement, and ultimately, adult quality of life' (2002b: 237) are encompassed. In order to increase the opportunities available to young Deaf people we need to incorporate this flexible notion of inclusion, recognizing that for some young people education in a residential school for the Deaf may signify inclusion in more social and learning opportunities, as may be equally true for inclusion in the mainstream for students with different needs.

Valuing Deaf Culture and the Deaf Community means that it is necessary to consider other lifestyles as 'successful' and other pathways as 'aspirational' (Watts, 2006: 311). It is all too easy to see young Deaf people's underachievement at school and levels of unemployment as evidence of lack of success or aspiration (Valentine and Skelton, 2007: 116). However, this is a biased perspective, measuring as it does 'Deaf people's participation within the hearing world rather than their self-identity and participation within Deaf culture' (ibid.: 116). There is a danger in assuming that all would want to be included in the current system and as Valentine and Skelton argue, 'For some Deaf people their experiences of the hearing world are either so negative and unrewarding, or so irrelevant in terms of their aspirations, that opting out of the hearing world is a positive choice (particularly from paid work in hearing environments or hearing educational environments)' (2007: 117).

Participation in mainstream educational opportunities may be accompanied by dilemmas and sacrifices. Does going to a mainstream school, college or university mean that young people have to give up their (sometimes hard won) Deaf identity? We need to consider ways in which to open up the present system to accommodate Deaf Culture in addition to providing much improved communication support facilities in mainstream institutions. Widening participation for this group is not straightforward and requires deconstruction of the current system. We also need to be wary of attempting to 'colonize' Deaf culture (Burke, 2002: 29). Inclusive education should avoid well-meaning attempts to assimilate young Deaf people into a mainstream culture.

Specialist provision or inclusion?

In this chapter we have been considering how issues to do with belonging and identity intersect with successful learning. These issues correspond with how and where Deaf young people should carry out their educations, whether in mainstream schools, colleges and universities, or in dedicated centres. At present there is only one university in the world which would claim to be fully immersed in Deaf Culture – Gallaudet University, in Washington, DC.

The university has been providing higher-level education to Deaf students in a full range of subjects for over 150 years. Throughout its history, Gallaudet has had to negotiate its relationship with the mainstream system and the hearing world. During the 1980s, faculty and staff protested the appointment of a hearing principal in the 'Deaf President Now' movement. This was a clear statement about Gallaudet's ability to excel without the paternalistic input of the hearing world. The Deaf activists won the symbolic battle to be educated in a system informed by Deaf Culture.

Protests were seen on campus in 2006 in a movement known as 'Unity for Gallaudet Now' in which students and faculty again disputed the board's choice of president. This recent debate also hinged on the relationship that Gallaudet should have with the hearing world. In an interview with the *Washington Post*, the retiring president, Jordan, stated that the protests were 'really about what it means to be a deaf person in the 21st century' (Hiatt, 2006). The protests were sparked by the comments of the proposed principal, Jane Fernandes, on the changing face of deafness. She is quoted as saying: 'More and more deaf babies now are getting cochlear implants, so that means more deaf children are hearing better and speaking better . . . That's the change that I represent, and it's scary for a lot of deaf people' (Hiatt, 2006). This was interpreted as a lack of support for Deaf Culture. Fernandes' vision for the future of Gallaudet welcomed students who came to Sign later in life, in addition to those with cochlear implants and those who had grown up in Deaf families, sometimes known as the Deaf elite. The protests can be interpreted as a conflict between those members of the Deaf Community who wished to retain Gallaudet's exclusive identity and those who saw the need to foster relationships with the hearing world.

There are other problems facing Gallaudet. In June 2007 the college was placed on probation by its accrediting body as a result of concerns regarding 'standards for leadership, academic rigor, student retention and integrity' *(Washington Post, 2007)*. Problems of exclusivity and multiple identities appear to make it hard for a Deaf institution to survive. Issues around the changing face of Deaf identity make it unclear what the experiences of the Deaf students of tomorrow will be and what support they will want.

A similar situation to the protests at Gallaudet University can be seen in the UK in the 2006 closure of Derby College for Deaf People. As with the situation with Gallaudet, inspectors raised problems to do with falling student numbers in addition to poor standards and leadership (Ofsted, 2003). The closure of the college was met with fierce protest and great sadness (*BBC News 24*, 2004a, 2004b). At a late stage in the discussions it was decided to integrate the college into the mainstream further education institution Derby College. The College for Deaf People became the 'Centre for Supported Learning', offering the opportunity for students to study at the mainstream college but live together in a residential setting (Derby Deaf Forum, 2005). The aim was to improve standards of teaching and access to the curriculum for Deaf students. Students can now take identical classes to hearing students at the college but with the opportunity to live in a supportive Deaf community. Access to the benefits of a mainstream education is facilitated by tailored linguistic support. A sign language video message on the Derby College website can be translated as 'Why do deaf people come to Derby College? Because there is good support in the college. This means deaf people can gain good qualifications and go to university or get a good job' (Derby College, 2007). The protests at the closure of the college for the Deaf were the result of mainstream standards conflicting with the desire to educate young Deaf people together. In Derby College it appears as if negotiations may have resulted in a positive outcome, in which the unique nature of Deaf experience is respected and nurtured alongside improved access to the benefits of a mainstream education.

Conclusion: learning with and from Deaf Culture

By questioning whose knowledge, culture and experience the current education system privileges and why, it becomes possible to negotiate alternative sources and styles of learning. There are potential mutual benefits from opening up communication between Deaf and hearing groups. Burke argues that we should be involved in 'engaging groups who have been socially excluded from participating in and contributing to the reconstruction of knowledge and meaning' (2002: 15). Some Deaf young people may opt out of mainstream education and culture altogether. For those who believe in education as a powerful tool to deconstruct dominant discourses, this can be an uncomfortable position to accept. However, as Watts argues, this needs to be respected as a valid choice, not an incidence of 'dropping out' or failure (2006: 309).

The potential for education systems to enact change from within, through dialogue with diverse groups, provides hope for working towards the goals of a pluralistic and inclusive society. Burke asks the crucial question: 'How might educational spaces be opened up to mobilise radical discourses and subject positions?' (2002: 10). The task for the education system should be to ask: How can we create and support spaces which incorporate, accept and promote learning from diversity? Differences such as modality of language may be accompanied by distinct ways of seeing and understanding the world, as in the case of Deaf signers, and these perspectives have much to offer. What might the current education system and mainstream society learn from such an interaction and what implicit values might be exposed that need to be challenged? These are the opportunities and challenges that thinking about Deaf young people in relation to inclusion and participation offer us.

Author's note

I first became interested in sign language and Deaf Culture when I was asked to help out at a summer school for 'profoundly deaf' children in 2001. I was told the children would be hard to handle because of the immense 'difficulties' they 'suffered' as a result of their condition but that they benefited enormously from the arts-based summer school. I was intrigued but apprehensive.

From my first day in the camp it became apparent that what I had been led to believe was way off the mark. I observed bright, articulate, sociable young people communicating with each other through a mixture of Sign language and speech, easily and creatively. They certainly did not seem to be the objects of pity I had been led to expect. Neither did they seem particularly grateful for the 'wonderful' opportunity given to them by the hearing staff at the camp to develop art, music and speech skills. In fact, like many young people, they were somewhat rebellious.

What quickly became obvious to me was the oppression they were under at the camp. I do not use that word lightly. It appeared to me as if their rights were constantly being violated. They were prohibited from signing to each other and instead were forced to speak. Their mobile phones, the means to stay in contact with friends and family at home, were confiscated so that they could not text. They were shouted at if they did not appear to be 'listening' or paying attention, often until they were in tears.

Back at home I began to read about Deaf history and Deaf education and I realized that what I had witnessed was indicative of the oppression experienced by Deaf people. This was the beginning of a journey for me that would involve learning British Sign Language, working as a communication support worker for Deaf students and writing a doctorate exploring aspects of Deaf Culture. What was apparent to me back then, and is still my motivation for research, is that no one has the right to oppress another's preferred language, their interests, or their culture and that young people appear to be particularly vulnerable to those who might dismiss their interests and identities as being without weight or without value. For me the goals of an inclusive society and the value of widening participation is not about making everyone the same but instead in valuing and celebrating difference.

Further reading

Lane, H. (1984), *When the Mind Hears*. New York: Random House.
Sacks, O. (1989), *Seeing Voices*. London: Picador.

References

BBC News 24 (2004a), 'Deaf students battle closure plans', 4 February. http: //news.bbc. co.uk/1/hi/england/derbyshire/3460391.stm (accessed 3 October 2007).

BBC News 24 (2004b), 'Deaf students lose out in closure', 11 February. http: //news.bbc. co.uk/1/hi/england/leicestershire/3478807.stm (accessed 3 October 2007).

Burke, P.J. (2002), *Accessing Education: Effectively Widening Participation.* Stoke-on-Trent: Trentham.

Conrad, R. (1979), *The Deaf School Child: Language and Cognitive Function.* London: Harper and Row.

Davis, L.J. (1997), 'Introduction: the need for disability studies', *The Disability Studies Reader.* London: Routledge.

Derby College: Achieving Success for Everyone (2007), 'Deaf Access'. www.derby-college. ac.uk/index.php?page=modules/DCSL/index.php&moduleID=DCSL (accessed 3 October 2007).

Derby Deaf Forum (2004), 'Derby College Centre for Supported Learning', 17 December. www. derbydeaf.co.uk/news.php (accessed 3 October 2007).

Derrida, J. (1974/1998), *Of Grammatology.* Translated by Gayatri Chakravorty. Reprint. Baltimore: Johns Hopkins University Press.

Dirksen, L. and Bauman, H.D.L. (1997), 'Toward a poetics of vision, space, and the body', *The Disability Studies Reader.* London: Routledge.

Hiatt, F. (2006), 'Signs of change at Gallaudet', *Washington Post*, 15 May. www.washingtonpost. com/wp-dyn/content/article/2006/05/14/AR2006051400805_pf.html (accessed 3 October 2007).

Ladd, P. (2003), *Understanding Deaf Culture: In Search of Deafhood.* Clevedon: Multilingual Matters.

Ofsted (2003), *Derby College for Deaf People.* http://preview.ofsted.gov.uk/reports/pdf/?inspe ctionNumber=299038&providerCategoryID=1048576&fileName=%5C%5Cschool%5C% 5C50%5C%5Cc00_50073_20061017.pdf (accessed 3 October 2007).

Powers, S. (2002a), 'The educational achievements of deaf school leavers', *Deafness @ Birth.* www.deafnessatbirth.org.uk/cgi-user/perlfect/search.pl?q=deaf&showurl=%2Fcontent2 %2Fpractice%2Fknow%2F04%2Findex.html (accessed 2 October 2007).

Powers, S. (2002b), 'From concepts to practice in deaf education: a UK perspective on inclusion', *Journal of Deaf Studies and Deaf Education*, 7, 230–243.

Powers, S., Gregory, S. and Thoutenhoofd, E.D. (1998), *The Educational Achievements of Deaf Children: A Literature Review.* London: DFES.

Sacks, O. (1989), *Seeing Voices.* London: Picador.

Valentine, G. and Skelton, T. (2007), 'Re-defining "norms": Deaf young people's transitions to independence', *The Sociological Review,* 55(1), 104–123.

Washington Post (2007), 'On Probation', 14 July. www.washingtonpost.com/wp-dyn/content/article/2007/07/13/AR2007071301894.html (accessed: 3 October 2007).

Watts, M. (2006), 'Disproportionate sacrifices: Ricoeur's theories of justice and the widening participation agenda for higher education in the UK', *Journal of Philosophy of Education*, 40(3), 301–312.

Wrigley, O. (1996), *The Politics of Deafness*. Washington, DC: Gallaudet University Press.

Freedom, Inclusion and Education

Joanna Haynes

Chapter Outline

Interpretations of freedom	77
Education and political liberation	80
Experimental and alternative education	81
Mainstream education: freedom through philosophical dialogue	85
Freedom to think	86
Conclusion	88
Author's note	89

This chapter is concerned with different interpretations of freedom and with exploring the connection between freedom and inclusion. Through critical pedagogy education can be a dynamic site for individual or collective action. I am particularly interested in educational approaches that emphasize the development of criticality as a means to address both social inclusion *and* freedom of thought and action. Criticality is also a way of positively engaging learners and teachers with the inevitable conflicts between competing rights and freedoms in a democratic society (Kelly, 1995). The chapter begins with a look at Fromm's seminal (1942) account of freedom. Drawing on the critical liberation pedagogy of Paulo Freire and the contributions of two educationalists who founded 'alternative' schools in the UK, notably A.S. Neill and J. Krishnamurti, the chapter then examines ideas about freedom at the site of education itself, touching very briefly on the critique of mass education made by deschoolers. Finally (and further developing ideas introduced in Chapter 2), some children's comments on their experiences of philosophical enquiry are included to illustrate a pedagogy that can create a space for experiences of freedom, criticality and community building in mainstream schools.

How can we be free to learn? If we want education to be participatory and accessible to all, debate about what freedom means, and the kind of pedagogy that provides learners and teachers with experiences of freedom, is to be expected. For those concerned with inclusion in education, the focus is on working to remove barriers and obstacles that interfere with freedom to learn. Such barriers can be practical, social, political or psychological. As well as challenging social inequalities, we need to understand the significance of relational and intra-personal dimensions of learning. Tony Brown discusses these aspects of learning in Chapter 3. The idea of *participation* in education is a political one and necessarily engages us with relationships between knowledge and power and discourses of plurality and difference. There is always a risk of indoctrination when the goals of education are expressly and instrumentally political. Making room for full participation in education implies commitment to an evolving, egalitarian and deliberative form of democracy: a society that refuses to accept inequality and that is open to the dialogue provoked by ongoing social change.

In talk of democracy, freedom of thought and expression, along with other forms of personal and political freedom, appear high on the list of what is most valued. The implication is that individual autonomy and freedom of choice add real quality to human experience, demonstrating the richness and complexity of what is possible for each person: choice creates an 'open future', a future to be designed, free from constraint or interference. Of course cultures vary in the degree to which the individual's wishes can or should be distinguished from the needs and wishes of the family or wider community group in determining the futures of its members. Contemporary Western culture tends to prize individualism above collectivism, but the defence of individual freedom does not have to be achieved at the expense of community building. Education is one of the spaces where values of autonomy and community might be put into practice. However, many would argue that there can be little choice or future for anyone without the essentials of life and education is very limited unless there is freedom from poverty, exploitation and fear.

Interpretations of freedom

Throughout his account of the history of freedom (*The Fear of Freedom*, first published in 1942), and particularly in the final chapter that discusses freedom and democracy, Fromm asks if freedom is not only the absence of external pressure but also the presence of something. He discusses two distinct forms of freedom: negative freedom (freedom from) and positive freedom (freedom to). This distinction between these two forms of liberty has been debated long and hard in political philosophy. Berlin (1969) argued that negative liberty is concerned with what a person should be left to do without interference. He suggested that positive liberty is preoccupied with the source of control that determines the choices a person makes either to do, or to be, one thing or another. Whilst negative freedom implies an *absence* of constraint, obstacles or interference that could inhibit choice or action, positive freedom is a *presence* of something that enables action, self-management and self-determination. If negative freedom is derived from *external* constraint, positive freedom (freedom to do something) emerges mainly from factors *internal* to an individual.

The liberal political tradition tends to emphasize the freedom of individuals and to favour laws that protect such liberties as freedom of expression, religion or travel. In his writing *On Liberty*, the English philosopher John Stuart Mill (1806–1873) argued that the only reason for preventing someone from doing something is that it harms someone else (the 'harm principle'). The difficulty here is interpreting the concept of harm. How harmful is it to tell a joke or draw a cartoon featuring a thick Irishman, a fanatical Christian or Muslim, a dumb blonde, a camp gay man? If some people are offended by the wearing of crucifixes or other religious symbols at work or school, is this a good reason for banning them? Mill also argued that individuals should have the right to express their beliefs freely. Should parents be free to send their children to a religious school? How might this affect the child's freedom to choose his or her religion? The issue of freedom to express beliefs gets more complicated when it involves the actions of children and young people and questions are asked about their competence to know their own beliefs or to make their own decisions. For example, if secondary school students decide it is important to join in anti-war protests taking place during the school day, should teachers, on the grounds of protecting their interests, try to prevent them from doing so, or discipline them for their absence from school? The issue of children's rights is discussed in Chapter 2.

Critical of the liberal viewpoint, Karl Marx (1818–1883) drew attention to the vital connection between freedom and equality, claiming that positive freedom is simply not possible without social equality. He argued that social class divisions under capitalism create human alienation and prevent self-realization. Marx believed that collective political action is the means for people to achieve and express positive freedom. Marx suggested that the state should sometimes act on behalf of citizens to ensure that one group or individual does not oppress, exploit or abuse another. It should constructively engineer greater equality to maximize positive freedom.

Free education is widely believed to be a social equalizer. In contemporary Western societies education is provided for free by the state, the young are 'protected' from child labour through compulsory schooling and arguably enabled to improve their later life chances. However, if a child goes to school every day inadequately nourished, he is not free to learn and realize his potential. Even if he is well nourished, he may go to school only to learn that, according to the school's standards or type of curriculum, he is regarded as a failure.

Is being poor the only factor in the experience of a lack of freedom? Some might argue that the wealthy are actually slaves to their possessions and life styles, and that this enslavement to material things is also at odds with authentic freedom. At an existential level, whether rich or poor, the persistence of desire itself can be experienced as a limitation of freedom (think of the consuming desire for chocolate, nicotine, alcohol and other drugs or cravings for comfort or attention). Taken further, the argument about the limiting effect of human desires echoes the idea that for freedom to exist, the passions must somehow be tamed or superseded. The conclusion of this line of thinking is that the liberation of a so-called higher self, through the practice of rationality or religious transcendence, is the true path to intellectual or spiritual freedom. Sensory pleasures do not feature at all in these highly rational or spiritual versions of the free life.

How might what we desire and what we consume shape our freedom? This is the moment to return to Fromm's account. In his study of the history of freedom, described as a history of growing individuation, Fromm takes into account the complex interrelationship between socio-economic, ideological and psychological factors in the pursuit of freedom. He is particularly concerned with what remains for us as human beings, once freedom from our preoccupation with basic survival or with external domination is established.

Fromm claims that 'human existence and freedom are from the beginning inseparable' (1942: 26), as man is always confronted with a choice between different courses of action. Acting against authority is a decidedly human act, suggests Fromm, and 'the act of disobedience as an act of freedom is the beginning of reason' (ibid.: 28). To what extent are educational institutions able to value disobedience as an act of freedom and to endorse this characterization of challenges to authority as the 'beginning of reason'? It would be surprising to see Fromm's account of disobedience as an act of freedom included in a school's discipline policy.

Fromm argues that our knowledge of our freedom leaves us with a sense of isolation, doubt and fear. He suggests that as social and cultural beings we tend to adopt certain 'mechanisms of escape' in the face of this fear. These are characterized in socio-psychological terms as responses of *authoritarianism*, *destructiveness* and *automaton conformity*. Fromm is concerned with these responses as part of a character structure expressing the basic experiences and mode of life common to most members of the group and he calls this the *social character* (1942: 239). Authoritarianism, he suggests, is derived from an overwhelming sense of powerlessness. Destructiveness is also derived from feelings of powerlessness as well as isolation, anxiety and a desire for self-preservation. In these modes, the individual overcomes feelings of insignificance by giving up his integrity or destroying others so that the world is no longer threatening (ibid.: 159). Automaton conformity is the 'escape' of choice by the majority and, in simple terms, is about renouncing the self to follow others and to 'blend in' to help overcome the anxiety of aloneness. Fromm argues that this form of escape leads the individual to what he calls *pseudo-acts* of thinking, feeling and willing (ibid.: 177), adopting a self that is not really his (ibid.: 220). Large institutions, including schools and workplaces, often seem to require this kind of conformity and subjugation of the self. It is not too difficult to recognize what Fromm terms 'mechanisms of escape' and 'pseudo acts' in contemporary culture and mass education among groups of teachers and learners alike: acts of avoidance and repetition.

Education and political liberation

So what kind of educational philosophy and practice might begin to address the relationship between social equality and freedom as well as the fear of freedom itself? A practising teacher as well as a writer, the Brazilian Paulo Freire's radical cultural politics (1985) draws on his experiences of adult literacy programmes in Latin America, North America and Africa. His vision of a liberated humanity and his theory of education are based on a view that relations of power in society are dialectical, never absolute, and these social relations always embody contradictions that could lead to alternative realities.

In Freire's optimistic philosophy, the social, cultural or economic constraints that people often experience simultaneously contain possibilities to be challenged or transformed: the seeds of change for the better. An awakening of consciousness is needed to enable the struggle for self-emancipation.

Freire was determined to challenge social and educational practices that served to maintain a culture of silence among the mass of people. Pedagogy itself had to be redesigned to reveal the logic of domination and exclusion. This was to be achieved by working within the history, discourses and experience of learners, particularly the traditionally excluded, and developing a language of transformation and possibility. These experiences offer material for investigation and debate and the opportunity to affirm and represent personal knowledge: a means to give presence and voice, rather than to silence learners.

Friere explains that for him teaching is a human act suggestive of certain qualities or characteristics in the teacher and in the classroom. He describes this as 'democratic authority' (1998: 86). It involves the teacher in being generous, respectful, open, just, ethical and committed. The teacher is not a technician delivering knowledge that is neutral and indifferent. Education is a profoundly political intervention.

Freedom is not the same as licence. It is not without limits. Friere characterizes the tension between freedom and authority in education thus:

> The great challenge for the democratic educator is how to transmit a sense of limit that can be ethically integrated by freedom itself. The more consciously freedom assumes its necessary limits, the more authority it has, ethically speaking, to continue to struggle in its own name.
>
> (1998: 96)

The question of how freedom of adults and children can be strengthened in the context of more democratic forms of education is a matter of profound interest to experimental and alternative educators.

Experimental and alternative education

In the mainstream world of education today, freedom is often dismissed as impractical or dangerous idealism, associated with the domains of a handful of 'alternative' individuals. For some it is forever locked in the progressive period of the 1960s, when a handful of free schools enjoyed a brief experimental honeymoon, breaching classroom boundaries, exploring alternative curricula and pedagogies and providing pupils with a major say in their learning and in the running of the school. Liverpool was the home to one such school where teachers and parents raised funds to take inner-city children on trips to parts of the country they had never visited, to look at the worlds beyond their neighbourhood and to observe the lives of others (BBC, 1993).

Education at the free school grew out of the desire to cut loose from the mass system and to be self-managing, to question the given curriculum and traditional relationships between teachers and students. The free-schoolers wanted to tap the interests of the pupils and enable them to be confident and self-educating. Although they attracted considerable local community support and involvement, the free schools were short-lived, unable to raise sufficient funds to pay everyday bills or to provide teachers with a living wage and unable to withstand the barrage of negative attention from the authorities in education and the media.

Experimental schools often accept young people who have been excluded or unable to 'fit in' elsewhere. Some attract those who are dissatisfied with mass education systems that emphasize narrow academic achievement and a certain brand of social advancement, rather than a wider range of intellectual, creative or practical abilities, knowledge and skills. Other alternative schools attract those who reject the social values of the most powerful and dominant groups in society. There are also those schools that emphasize sustainability and life skills, where education is managed in a more localized way and on a smaller scale, such as the Human Scale Education (www.hse.org.uk). Experimental schools often cause controversy and attract media attention.

It is difficult to evaluate such educational 'experiments' in today's performance-related terms. They are often small scale, selective and socially unrepresentative in their intake. They argue, understandably, that they should not be measured by the same criteria as other schools since they do not set out to achieve the same ends. One approach to evaluation is to consider the outcomes at a later point in the lives of students and to allow those people to speak for themselves. Another approach is to attempt to measure other 'value' added by the school, such as health and wellbeing, which Alan Hutchison (Chapter 6) suggests is something with which education should be concerned. However their impact is measured, there is much to be learned from alternative and experimental schools and their differences often help to stimulate wider debate about the purposes of education. Two such schools are discussed below.

Case study: choosing to learn

Occasionally referred to dismissively as the 'do as you please school', Summerhill is a famous educational community featured in a docu-drama on children's television (CBBC TV, 2007). Founded in 1921, by A.S. Neill, there are currently about ninety children and twelve full-time staff. Children can attend from the age of five and the oldest students are about seventeen. The school has always strongly advocated personal freedom for students, viewing this as necessary to the discovery of self within the safety of a democratic self-governing community in which all members are equal citizens. A fundamental tenet of Neill's philosophy is that education is living and living is education.

Summerhill is unique in offering students the freedom to choose whether or not to attend lessons. It was this founding principle that was challenged by a team of school inspectors in 1999 and resulted in a long legal battle by the school to retain the principle that lessons should be voluntary, rather than compulsory. Newman (in Kassem et al., 2006) has written an informative account of this episode in the school's history along with discussion of the current culture of public auditing. The fundamental principle of Summerhill's trusting educational philosophy is that each of us must drive our own life and learning and that all are capable of such responsibility: the first step in developing intrinsic motivation and achieving so-called 'personalized learning'. In interviews with 16- to 17-year-old students, conducted as part of the school's building of a case for non-compulsory lessons, interviewees speak of confidence, being oneself, independence, responsibility to self and others, tolerance, freedom and self-government as some of the qualities they most value in their Summerhill education (www.summerhillschool.co.uk/pages/pupil-interviews.html).

A major cornerstone of Summerhill's community life is the weekly meeting, where all rules and decisions are made and where each person, whether adult or child, has an equal say. This represents a very serious commitment to democratization of the school community and goes much further than school councils in mainstream schools, which are sometimes rather tokenistic and limited forms of consultation. Summerhill's educational practice recognizes both freedom of individual expression and freedom to participate in decision making as aspects of voice within a community.

Neill was not interested in politics, only in the lives of children. He believed that compulsory schooling had a fundamentally limiting effect on children's development as independent learners, and on children's rights and ability to make decisions and to act on them as well as a harmful and distorting impact on relationships between and among adults and children. In this regard he shared territory with the de-schoolers.

Illich's seminal *Deschooling Society* (1973) argued that schools are outdated, unrealistic learning environments, inefficient in their monopoly of resources and buildings, indoctrinating and killing enthusiasm for learning through the imposition of timetables, the segregation of children into age and attainment-determined groups and the separation of subject matter. He claimed that the system of awarding qualifications is a persuasive method of natural selection and weeding out, hiding behind a myth of equality. Holt put forward the idea of 'learned failure' among the excluded, and suggested that schools are 'designed and built not to move them (poor children) up in the world but to keep them at the bottom of it and to make them think it is their fault' (1972: 186). The de-schoolers were concerned with wider social change and advocated education through the development of learning networks.

Educationalist Jidhu Krishnamurti (1895–1986) believed that education could bring about positive social change. He was interested in intellectual freedom, something that he felt is bound up with the cultivation of mental awareness and perception, with the ways in which minds are 'conditioned' and fear disposes us to cling to particular beliefs and ideologies. His conception of intellectual freedom seems to bring together the holistic and embodied notion of 'mindfulness' associated with Eastern philosophies with the Western tradition of critical thinking. Krishnamurti was deeply concerned by divisiveness in all its forms and wanted students to engage critically with all social, religious, parental and traditional influences (Dewhurst, 1994).

Case study: freedom and social change

Founded by Krishnamurti in 1969, Brockwood Park School expresses two key aims pertaining to freedom: to explore what freedom and responsibility are in relationship with others and in modern society and to see the possibility of being free from self-centred action and inner conflict (www.brockwood.org.uk). These aims address both political and psychological dimensions of freedom. Deep discussion is a crucial part of life and learning in schools such as Brockwood Park, and topics are wide ranging. Krishnamurti exemplified the approach in his writing (Lutyens, 1990) and his work as a public speaker. It was often his way, when invited to address an audience, to arrive without any notes and start to speak, working from the freshest thinking, continuously seeking to provoke and challenge his own mind to speak freely, without resort to emotional, social or intellectual refuges, to engage attention and awareness. He regarded this degree of openness as necessary to genuine dialogue.

Krishnamurti's exchanges with David Bohm helped to inspire Bohm's *On Dialogue*, in which he defines true dialogue as 'a stream of meaning flowing among us and through us' (1995: 6). Bohm explains his view of the vital connections

⇨

between democratic and dynamic forms of dialogue and the generation of new knowledge thus:

> Communication can lead to the creation of something new only if people are able freely to listen to each other, without prejudice, and without trying to influence each other . . . Each has to be interested primarily in truth and coherence, so that he is ready to drop his old ideas and intentions and be ready to go onto something different, when this is called for.
>
> (1995: 3)

For both Neill and Krishnamurti, freedom is not about seeking self-gratification at the expense of others. Echoing Fromm, it involves confronting various fears, habits and attachments. Fear and compulsion obstruct intelligence and independence of mind. Like Friere, both argue that teachers require understanding of the deep motivation and psychology of authority, domination and the nurturing of dependence in the pedagogical relationship. Both writers offer insights into the relationship between learning and the intellectual, emotional, psychological and political dimensions of freedom. In these perspectives on learning, it is the dynamic process of dialogue with others that serves not only to educate but also to regulate the distribution of power in the life of the educational community.

Mainstream education: freedom through philosophical dialogue

What about practices of freedom in the majority of schools? Philosophy for children (Lipman, 1991, 1993) aims to develop criticality, reasonableness and practical wisdom through questioning, enquiry and collaborative dialogue in classrooms. Through this pedagogy, learners contribute directly to the creation of knowledge and classes develop as participatory communities. In a philosophy session, students' questions form the agenda and the group engage in a cyclical process of dialogue and reflection, a process described as a community of enquiry. It is an open-ended, tactful, challenging, responsive pedagogy, in which the outcomes are not known in advance, in strong contrast with scripted lessons that have predefined objectives. A case study of one first school where philosophy for children is part of the practice of strengthening children's voices was outlined in Chapter 2.

Stories of doing philosophy recounted by children from Gallions Primary School in the East End of London also give food for thought about the role of freedom in education. A group of 10 and 11 year olds had been invited to speak about their perspectives on philosophical enquiry to an audience of some 120 educators at a conference I attended in 2006. Following their presentations they invited questions from the audience. When someone asked 'If there was no philosophy, what would school be like?' one of the boys in the group replied: 'It would be like a black and white film. Philosophy adds the detail and colour.' To this striking metaphor of his school experience he added: 'At school, mostly teachers take over the lesson plans . . . in philosophy, children take over the lesson plan, and sometimes you don't even need a lesson plan.'

Another girl in the group agreed that philosophy is not a lesson at all, but a time for expressing ideas, when you could start with one thing and end up somewhere else. One student referred to the sense of relief associated with 'letting opinions and feelings out' and several children mentioned the calming effects of doing philosophy. The children also described philosophy as something that can be done anywhere and is part of everyday life.

Jason told the audience that he would have a lot more emotional turmoil if it were not for the philosophy sessions, because they provided a time and space, not only to express thoughts and feelings, but also to consider their effects and consequences. He told the audience that philosophy is what makes it possible for him to go to school and he described its position in his life in this way: 'You've got home and you've got school, and philosophy is sort of in between.'

Watching and listening to their presentation, you could not fail to be deeply impressed by the poise and thoughtfulness of these young people. Their relaxed and natural confidence created a sense of curiosity. They had considered what they intended to say, but this was not a scripted delivery. They responded to questions from the audience with a delightful mixture of humour, openness and authority.

Freedom to think

The presentation exhibited the children's sense of freedom and power and demonstrated just how articulate such experiences of learning can enable young people to be. Their accounts alluded to both senses of the idea of freedom: negative freedom (freedom from lesson plans or the teacher giving the answers), as well as opportunities to pursue personal autonomy, flourishing and self-realization in the school community (freedom to play with ideas, and to listen to others or to change your mind), positive freedom.

The pupils at Gallions Primary felt free to say what they thought and to let one another speak and express emotion. They enjoyed sessions of philosophical enquiry that did not follow a pre-set course and where they could genuinely influence the direction of dialogue. Such openness can create anxiety for some teachers when authentic questioning pushes at the boundaries of comfort or introduces controversy (Haynes, 2005). However, if we want pupils to develop scepticism and independence of thought, such authenticity is essential. Doddington argues that an over-emphasis on rules interferes with learning and advocates the provision of opportunities for authentic conversation in education:

> Talking is a fundamental form of expression for each individual located 'between' persons as conversation. It is the basic vehicle for personal engagement with others and serves to develop thought and identity.
>
> (2001: 273)

The word 'letting' cropped up several times in Gallions students' reports of their philosophical conversations: letting one's own ideas out, letting go of the predetermined lesson plan, letting each other speak. Doing philosophy seemed to allow a relinquishing of routine constraints and habits. They relished the power of ways of thinking and deliberating that they could bring to bear on their everyday lives. These liberating conditions powered their urges to think. The removal of certain constraints appeared to unleash their powers of creative thinking. They felt free to play with words and ideas. They welcomed the protected time and space to explore issues that might otherwise be unmanageably troublesome.

These children from Gallions Primary were certainly making their voices heard, both in the sense of drawing on interpretations of philosophy and using language inventively to create vivid expressions of their unique selves, in speaking, writing and in other forms, and in the sense of participating in a dynamic and inventive social activity that was evidently making a positive difference, not only to their classroom community, but also beyond. In the teaching resource *Thinking Allowed* (Gallions Primary School, 2007) pupils and teachers from Gallions Primary claim that philosophizing with one another has provided them with the means to address both questions and conflicts that arise at other times. The idea of 'voice' in education, particularly the voice of child, is discussed in Chapter 2.

The themes of freedom from routine, freedom from turmoil and ridicule, and freedom to explore questions arising from everyday life are echoed in my own practice of philosophy with primary school children. Children are keen to learn ways to free themselves from distraction and to improve their ability to relax and concentrate in order to think, listen and learn effectively. Students truly value acceptance, impartiality and being listened to by each other and by adults (Haynes, 2002: 54–5, 61–2). This is partly because it remains an experience that is still quite rare and unaccustomed for them. However, it is not just pupils who relish this calm atmosphere of mutual respect and absence of constraint. Teachers also describe the sense of liberation they experience when they first participate in philosophical enquiry themselves and the avenues of thinking that children open up for them through their philosophical questions (BBC, 1990). They describe some initial fear of the open space of unscripted teaching followed by a sense of release and excitement as they learn the role of philosophical facilitator, listening to children's thinking and responding in the moment. Judging from the responses reported here, certain freedoms can positively transform the classroom experience, for learners and teachers alike.

That such freedom to think and talk is worthy of note by teachers and pupils alike is a little worrying, given the value that our culture claims to place on freedom of thought and expression and on traditions of critical thinking and democratic process. However, it is pretty rare these days to find the words freedom and learning alongside one another. The notion of freedom as a precious potential outcome of education, as a desirable part of the educational experience and as a necessary condition of learning and human development, is rather neglected. In the light of reports from students and teachers, such as those from Gallions Primary, it is worth reconsidering this ranking and the part that freedom plays in enabling us to distinguish education from schooling.

Conclusion

Fromm's work draws together the social and existential dimensions of human freedom. Through the work of practising educationalists such as Freire, Neill, Krishnamurti and Lipman discussed in this chapter, we can begin to see in practice what might be required to create conditions in education for freedom of thought and expression and for transformation towards social inclusion.

This is pedagogy that encourages criticality and dialogue and provides authentic opportunities for the exercise of choice and participation in education, including schools. Respect, openness, listening and dialogue are core ingredients in this form of education as encounter. From such examples we can imagine the possibility of education *through* democracy, education as an *experience of* democracy, as a space of spontaneity, rather than repetition, in which it is possible for learners and teachers freely to take initiative and to act (Biesta, 2006: 138).

Author's note

As the child of an itinerant family, I attended many schools in different parts of the world. I soon found out that school was not one thing, and that experience for pupils could vary hugely according to the ethos of the school, and according to the individual teacher. Like most children, I understood that schools were places of authority and that teachers had great power. I learned to be very observant and curious about life in classrooms as I moved from school to school and this is where my concern with educational relationships was born.

As a philosophy undergraduate in the early 1970s, I read Fromm's *Fear of Freedom* in my first year at university and we read Ivan Illich's *Deschooling Society* in class soon after it was published. Its critique of schools and relationships between teachers and students made a strong impression and sowed the seeds of my lifelong interest in critical pedagogy and ideas of freedom in education.

References

BBC (1990), 'Socrates for Six Year Olds', *The Transformers*, London: BBC TV. Available as *Communities of Enquiry* DVD produced by SAPERE. www.sapere.net

BBC (1993), *Education Special: Lessons in Freedom*. London: BBC TV.

Berlin, I. (1969), *Four Essays on Liberty*. Oxford: Oxford University Press.

Biesta, G. (2006), *Beyond Learning: Democratic Education for a Human Future*. London: Paradigm.

Bohm, D. (1995), *On Dialogue*. Edited by Lee Nichol. London: Routledge.

Brockwood Park School, www.brockwood.org.uk

CBBC TV (2007), *Summerhill*. London: BBC TV.

Dewhurst, D. (1994), 'Awareness of mind: a discussion of the Krishnamurti schools in India', *Educational Philosophy and Theory*, 26(2), 16–32.

Doddington, C. (2001), 'Entitled to speak: talk in the classroom', *Studies in Philosophy and Education*, 20, 267–274.

Gallions Primary School (2007), *Thinking Allowed: Philosophy for Children at Gallions Primary School*. Gallions Primary School, Beckton, London.

Freire, P. (1985), *The Politics of Education: Culture, Power and Liberation*. Basingstoke and London: Macmillan.

Freire, P. (1998), *Pedagogy of Freedom: Ethics, Democracy and Civic Courage*. Lanhan, MD: Rowman and Littlefield.

Fromm, E. (1942), *Fear of Freedom*. London: Routledge and Kegan Paul.

Haynes, J. (2002), *Children as Philosophers: Learning through Enquiry and Dialogue in the Primary School*. London: RoutledgeFalmer.

Haynes, J. (2005), 'The costs of thinking', *Teaching Thinking and Creativity*, 17, 32–37.

Holt, J. (1972), *Freedom and Beyond*. New York: Dutton and Co.

Human Scale Education, www.hse.org.uk.

Illich, I. (1973), *Deschooling Society*. Harmondsworth: Penguin.

Kassem, D., Mufti, E. and Robinson, J. (2006), *Education Studies: Issues and Critical Perspectives*. Maidenhead: Open University Press.

Kelly, A.V. (1995), *Education and Democracy: Principles and Practices*. London: Paul Chapman.

Lipman, M. (1991), *Thinking in Education*. Cambridge: Cambridge University Press.

Lipman, M. (ed.) (1993), *Thinking, Children and Education*. Dubuque, IA: Kendall/Hunt.

Lutyens, M. (ed.) (1990), *The Krishnamurti Reader*. Harmondsworth: Penguin Arcana.

Mill, J.S. (1982), *On Liberty*. Harmondsworth: Penguin.

Neill, A.S. (1985), *Summerhill*. London: Pelican.

Summerhill School, www.summerhillschool.co.uk/pages/pupil-interviews.html (accessed 15 February 2008).

Wellbeing and Education

Alan Hutchison

Chapter Outline

The idea of wellbeing	92
What is wellbeing education?	92
Why wellbeing education now?	93
Problematizing wellbeing education	98
Critical voices	98
Contemporary developments in wellbeing	99
Conclusion	101
Author's note	101

> [T]he central purpose of education is to promote human flourishing.
>
> (Brighouse, 2006: 42)

This chapter is informed by a commitment to educational practice as a positive and emancipatory experience for all learners. It raises questions about the existing economic, social, cultural and educational order, through its focus on wellbeing, and agrees with Goodley's suggestion that 'an exploration of inclusion involves an exposition of the cultures and societies in which education is enacted' (Goodley, 2007: 4).

Following some conceptual ground clearing, the chapter focuses on the case for wellbeing education. Attention is then given to critical voices on wellbeing education before examining a range of current developments in the UK and elsewhere. The chapter concludes that wellbeing education should be a focus for all concerned with educational debate, policy and practice.

The idea of wellbeing

Wellbeing can be defined as 'a state of being with others, where human needs are met, where one can act meaningfully to pursue one's goals and where one enjoys a satisfactory quality of life' (Newton, 2007: 1). The UK government sees wellbeing as a 'positive physical, social and mental state; it is not just the absence of pain, discomfort and incapacity. It requires that basic needs are met, that individuals have a sense of purpose, that they feel able to achieve personal goals and participate in society' (ibid.: 1).

A recent review of literature concluded 'there is no accepted definition of 'wellbeing' (Hird, 2003: 4). However, we might be able to make some progress in distinguishing 'objective' measures of wellbeing from 'subjective' measures of wellbeing.

> Objective wellbeing might be examined through the following measurements:
>
> - the percentage of children aged 15 reporting less than ten books in their home
> - the percentage of 15 to 19 year olds staying on in education or training
> - or the percentage of 15 to 19 year olds not in education, training or employment.

These are examples of measures included in recent research on wellbeing (UNICEF, 2007) and, as Newton argues, 'this covers the level of wealth, provision of education and health care, infrastructure and so on' (ibid.: 2). On the other hand, 'subjective' wellbeing is more concerned with how people *feel* about their lives and experiences. This is more concerned with people's own sense of happiness, as against some measurement of their resources or participation in education and training. In what follows, I shall use the term 'happiness' to indicate my interest in the subjective sense of wellbeing.

What is wellbeing education?

Wellbeing education focuses on human happiness and seeks to promote what Aristotle called 'eudaimonia', emphasizing human flourishing (Noddings, 2005: 10) rather than simply promoting the pursuit of pleasure. People flourish when they are engaged in the world they participate in and have a significant sense of meaningfulness in their lives. On the other hand, pleasure might be thought of as a more transient experience, often related to the satisfaction of the senses, such as visual or physical experience.

Wellbeing education attempts to rejuvenate a debate about values, what is considered to be important in contemporary society, the institutions which operate within it and the purposes which are intended to guide the detailed processes of educational experience. It commits us to the value of wellbeing as a central principle to guide the construction of educational life. It looks to scientific and philosophical perspectives for clues to understand happiness and makes use of empirical studies to assess the value of practices advocated in its name. Pedagogically, wellbeing education values the experiences of all pupils and students as a basis for educational practice; thus, the voices of all learners figure centrally in such processes. From this perspective, the efforts of schools and other institutions are to be judged partly on the basis of whether they have managed to equip pupils and students with an ability to understand what does and does not contribute to a happy life.

Why wellbeing education now?

As Noddings has observed, 'people want to be happy and, since this desire is well-nigh universal, we would expect to find happiness as an aim of education' (2005: 74). However, we might question how far this is indeed the case in our education systems.

According to Layard (2005, 2007), a key advocate for happiness as a central value for education, many contemporary societies seem to have an excessive preoccupation with the economic aspects of life and especially with the promotion of a growing economy. The logic seems to be that with an increasingly globalized economy it is imperative that nations use their human resources as effectively as they can to ensure they are able to compete with other nations. Crucially, this means that the skills and qualifications of workers are developed as far as they can be. This idea also links with a key concept developed in recent years which has taken root in many educational systems, including the British one, namely the idea of 'lifelong learning'. This suggests that the need to compete with other countries in a global economy involves removing the idea that education is something which comes to an end for people after compulsory schooling. Instead, the emphasis is that education should continue throughout one's life. Moreover, the growth of policies concerned with the theme of 'widening participation', in the UK, for example, seem to be concerned with issues such as how to overcome barriers to participation in education and training and how to stimulate interest in such experience among those who have not previously had access to higher education. Some discourses around 'participation' seem to neglect a critical examination of the purposes of participation. What is neglected in these discourses is an engagement with learning for life, or indeed learning as living and living as learning where the whole person's wellbeing is regarded as an essential focus for educational practice. The critical question of what can constitute barriers in education is exemplified further in Haynes, in Chapter 5 of this book.

Noddings has argued that, until quite recently, talk about the aims of education 'figured prominently in educational theory and most education systems prefaced their curriculum documents with statements of their aims' (2005: 74) and she rightly ponders what might have been lost by a relative neglect of 'aims-talk'.

Interestingly, a growing body of evidence is pointing to the hollowness of claims that growing material prosperity can provide a sustained basis for improvements in people's wellbeing (Newton, 2007). Layard's evidence indicates that improvements in material living standards, as measured by real income per head over the past fifty years, do not relate to any real sustained improvement in human happiness.

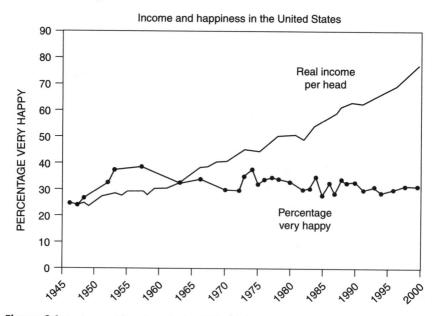

Figure 6.1 Income and happiness in the US (Layard, 2005: 30)

Of course, we should be alert to any problems in making these kinds of measurements (Oswald, 2007), but nevertheless such evidence does raise serious questions about the primacy of economic productivity and consumerism as the basis for a fulfilling life.

Moreover, a different type of evidence dwells upon the different values held by people and how these might be related to wellbeing. As Layard points out, 'excessive focus on financial rewards can . . . reduce happiness . . . the people who care most about money are less happy with a given amount of it than other people are' (2005: 141). Indeed, a growing empirical literature seems to be pointing to the high price paid by a commitment to materialism in relation to mental health and general wellbeing (Kasser, 2002; Kasser and Kanner, 2004).

If we accept the claim that, beyond a certain level, increased affluence really does have little impact upon happiness, some explanation is required. One such explanation has been suggested by Haidt (2006), who argues that changes in people's material livings conditions, such as increased income and spending power, are subject to a psychological process he calls 'the adaptation principle' (ibid.: 84). Basically, as we improve our living standards, we quickly come to take this as our point of reference and then find ourselves striving for the next lot of improvements. In this sense, we may find ourselves stuck on what Haidt refers to as the 'hedonic treadmill' (ibid.: 86). As he puts it:

> On an exercise treadmill you can increase the speed all you want, and accumulate all the riches, fruit trees, and concubines you want, but you can't get ahead . . . the riches you accumulate will just raise your expectations and leave you no better off than before. Yet, not realizing the futility of our efforts, we continue to strive . . . always wanting more than we have, we run and run and run, like hamsters on a wheel.
>
> (ibid.: 86)

Interestingly, these kinds of arguments resonate with a number of other philosophical and religious traditions (Schoch, 2007). For example, Gandhian writers (Kumar, 2004) would argue Western societies have lost their way in terms of their cultural emphasis upon 'having' rather than 'being'. (Haynes also touches on this theme in her discussion of interpretations of freedom in Chapter 5.) That is, the apparent preoccupation with materialism as the basis for wellbeing is misplaced and unsustainable. In its place, a much more holistic emphasis is proposed where the good of others, and indeed of the environment, is valued. Buddhist perspectives also seem to point to the insidious nature of desire and the value of developing awareness of the way the mind constructs reality ('mindfulness') and cultivating an attitude of loving-kindness towards others, as against an acquisitive materialism (Sumedho, 2007).

The value of wellbeing education seems to be implicit in the work of many critical theorists. Drawing upon the work of Marcuse, Brookfield suggests that:

> In advanced industrial society, the most pernicious oppression of all is that of affluence. Lulled into stupefaction by the possession of consumer goods, we believe ourselves to believing in democratic freedom, when our needs have actually been manipulated to convince us we are happy. In reality, a condition of disaffection lurks beneath the [surface] of everyday life. If we could just see our alienated state clearly, we would want to liberate ourselves from it.
>
> (Brookfield, 2006: 189)

How far does contemporary educational experience equip children and young people to critically evaluate the way capitalist societies require their citizens to engage in the relentless pursuit of material goods, thus maintaining profitability of the economy? Equality and social justice seem to have slipped off the political and educational agenda. Moreover, the individualistic emphasis of such societies seems to have corroded social relationships and, according to writers such as Putnam, has resulted in an unprecedented collapse in community and associational life in the United States in the last forty years, with serious negative consequences. Putnam (2000) argues that virtually every traditional civic, social and fraternal organization – typified by bowling leagues – has undergone a considerable reduction in membership at the same time as the number of people bowling had increased drastically. For Putnam, the key dimension of human experience lost in this process is what he calls 'social capital', which is to do with the value of belonging to social networks, with relationships with others. Commenting on a radio programme on the social damage produced by television, Putnam says, 'People watch *Friends* on TV – they don't have them' (NPR, 2007). The claim is that social capital is a vital component of people's wellbeing, a claim reinforced by empirical studies developed by the emerging field of 'positive psychology' (Seligman et al., 2005). Hence, the increasingly individualized nature of contemporary life, reinforced by much educational and training experience, may be pushing people away from improving their wellbeing.

There is a need to improve social relationships and the social trust which goes with them. Certainly, some recent evidence suggests there has been a worrying decrease in social trust over a relatively short time. Layard claims that:

> there has been an extraordinary fall in trust [in Britain and the United States] since 1960 from roughly 56% of the population trusting most other people to only 30% today. Levels of trust in Britain are particularly low among young people: only a quarter say 'yes' when asked if they trust most other people (Park et al., 2004). By contrast, there has been no fall in trust in any other European country since 1981 when the data were first collected.
>
> (2007: 19)

Layard's explanation for this is clearly focused on the 'huge growth of individualism in the United States, which has washed across the Atlantic like a tsunami, hitting Britain first and the rest of Europe much less, so far' (2007: 20).

Moreover, the highly individualized and competitive nature of social life in contemporary capitalist societies may form the basis for negative influences on our wellbeing. Some commentators have drawn attention to the key role played by an excessive concern with social comparison and image in damaging our subjective wellbeing. De Graaf and colleagues suggest that:

> The daily bombardment of advertising images leaves us forever dissatisfied with our own appearance and that of our real-life partners. . . . it encourages us to meet our non-material needs through material ends . . . it tells us to buy their product because we'll be loved, we'll be accepted. . . . it tells us that we are not lovable and acceptable without buying their product. . . . To be lovable and acceptable is to have the right image. Authenticity be damned.
>
> (2005: 157)

Do our educational practices provide pupils and students with the critical understanding needed to interrogate pervasive economic and cultural assumptions about what makes for a happy life? This is especially pressing now since work in Positive Psychology is suggesting it is possible to increase people's wellbeing (Seligman et al., 2005). The details of some of this work will be touched on more fully later in this chapter.

Finally, the case for wellbeing education can also be made through an examination of evidence on the absence of wellbeing. James (1998) has written at length about what he sees as the dramatic rise in unhappiness in Britain since the 1950s and other writers have charted a considerable rise in emotional problems in recent years:

> Evidence for Britain certainly indicates big rises in emotional disturbance. For example, the proportion of 16-year-olds with serious emotional problems rose

from 10% in 1986 to 17% in 1999 (Collishaw et al., 2004) . . . and the latest research by Stephan Collishaw and his colleagues shows things have continued to worsen.

(Layard, 2007: 19)

In light of the above, there exists considerable evidence for the argument that wellbeing education deserves closer examination by policy makers, practitioners and those being educated. Knowler also argues in Chapter 7 that much greater attention needs to be paid to young people's sense of belonging in supporting their inclusion in education.

Problematizing wellbeing education

Having started the construction of a case for wellbeing education, there are a number of issues which need to be examined in moving towards the development and implementation of any initiatives. For example, there are issues to consider around the appropriation of the concept 'wellbeing' by those with particular vested economic or political interests. Interestingly, politicians of both major political parties in Britain have welcomed the focus upon happiness; for example, the conservative leader, David Cameron, has spoken on his concern about wellbeing (*Daily Telegraph*, 2007) and has set up a 'Children's Taskforce' to investigate. We must nevertheless bear in mind that politicians are not experts on education or psychology and any proposals emerging from this sector need to be considered critically. There are other issues around the politics of a wellbeing curriculum, including who might decide and whether there would be agreement on the key constituents of the programme. There are issues to consider around the timing of programmes and the stages at which learners might engage with particular themes and issues, let alone young people's participation in the introduction and content of any such programme Moreover, people's lives are hugely shaped by their experience outside formal educational institutions and the role of informal contexts in contributing to wellbeing needs also to be recognized.

Critical voices

Despite the arguments, evidence and enthusiasm of proponents of wellbeing education, some critics have voiced substantial concerns. As the Midlands Psychology Group point out, citing the work of Frank Furedi (2003), 'so much of our popular culture – from reality TV programmes to most of the counselling and psychotherapy industry – encourages us to believe that we can change our lives at will, given enough therapeutic insight and motivation' (Midlands Psychology Group, 2007: 423). These writers want to point to the 'social and material world with which we are intimately connected' (ibid.) in highlighting the importance of the objective influences on wellbeing, such as employment, income, housing, health etc. Clearly these aspects should not be lost sight of in any consideration of social policy and are recognized in the broad definitions of wellbeing mentioned above. The critics make their position clear in suggesting that:

> It is perhaps not overstating things to say that the current official preoccupa-
> tion with 'happiness' amounts at best to a naïve attempt to improve the world
> through wishful thinking, and at worst to a form of insidious social control,
> where people are encouraged to look inwards for the sources of their troubles,
> and in the end to implicitly blame themselves for these ills.
>
> (ibid.: 425)

Likewise, Ecclestone (2007) questions whether attending to the wellbeing of students is supported by any convincing evidence and she asserts that 'inserting a vocabulary of emotional vulnerablilty into education is likely to encourage the very feelings of depression and hopelessness it is supposed to deal with'.

I would encourage the reader to consider these kinds of arguments in coming to a view about the value of wellbeing education. Such opinions do not seem to have inhibited the recent worldwide interest in the issue of wellbeing and related educational developments, some of which have been subject to careful empirical scrutiny as discussed in the following section.

Contemporary developments in wellbeing

A popular programme at Harvard University is Tal Ben-Shahar's Positive Psychology course (Ben-Shahar, 2006). Cambridge University has recently established its own Wellbeing Institute (www.cambridgewellbeing.org) to advance the scientific understanding of wellbeing and its application to people and institutions. A number of substantial books have been produced (Huppert et al., 2005) and their work also involves developing materials for use in the classroom by teachers and secondary school students. A number of programmes have been developed for use with school children, including the

Penn Resilience Project, designed by Professor Martin Seligman, the founder of Positive Psychology. In this project, 11-year-old students spend eighteen classroom hours on such issues as understanding their own emotions and those of others and developing concern for others, taught by a specially trained teacher. Eleven different evaluation studies have been undertaken on the programme and 'except in one school where the training was inadequate, it has reduced the rate of teenage depression over the next three years by on average one half' (Layard, 2007: 20–1). In Britain, a much publicized programme has been developed at Wellington College, a large fee-paying private school, where:

> girls and boys in years 10 and 11 (aged 14+ and 15+) will have a 40-minute timetabled lesson on 'the skills of well-being' every fortnight for two years. The lessons will give them an understanding of what factors help a life to thrive and flourish, as well as teaching them some practical skills for everyday use.
>
> The unique curriculum has been devised for Wellington by Dr Nick Baylis of the University of Cambridge (www.cambridgewellbeing.org), one of the world's leading specialists in the science of well-being. The approach is founded on the principle of studying lives that go particularly well, and then using that knowledge to develop and apply strategies and skills that promote all-round progress in a person's psychological, physical and social life. Importantly, the curriculum takes a rounded approach to the subject of life development, combining a core of positive psychology with teaching on a range of other key factors such as sleep, nutrition and exercise. Ten of the school's existing teachers are being trained to deliver the curriculum, led by Wellington's Ian Morris, who has devised the classroom applications in close collaboration with Dr Baylis.
>
> (Wellington College, 2007)

The UK government's own SEAL (Social and Emotional Aspects of Learning) project (DfES, 2007) increasingly influences educational practice and the concept of 'emotional intelligence' (Goleman, 1996) is providing a focus for such educational developments. These have been subject to significant criticisms (Craig, 2007). Other projects are also being developed in consultation with educational experts and teachers by making use of the Buddhist concept of 'mindfulness' and a 'Mindfulness Education programme' is now in use in the Vancouver school system in Canada and will be in Minnesota and New York in January 2008 (Hawn Foundation, 2007). There has been a growth in what could be described as the 'slow movement', which is questioning the frenetic, over-commercialized and hollow practices which have become so embedded in much of Western culture. Honore's book,

In Praise of Slow (2004), which has become a best-seller, suggests that a world-wide movement is challenging the 'cult of speed'. In other academic work, the theory of post-materialism has been proposed, suggesting an ongoing transformation of individuals and society which liberates them gradually from the stress of basic acquisitive or materialistic needs (Inglehart, 1971).

Conclusion

There appears to be a considerable growth worldwide of interest in states of happiness and the role that educational experience might play in these. In part, this interest has developed as a result of growing awareness that a preoccupation with economic prosperity and a consumer-oriented lifestyle may not provide an adequate context for a flourishing, happy life. In his most recent work, Layard (2007) has called for teachers to be trained to teach values and the ways to happiness. Happiness and wellbeing are critical issues in the provision of an engaging, inclusive education.

For further exploration

1. Watch online videos featuring some of the leading figures in wellbeing research and practice shown in a BBC series *The Happiness Formula* in 2006: http://news.bbc.co.uk/1/hi/programmes/happiness_formula/4771908.stm

Then consider the following questions:
- What is happiness?
- Scientists claim that happiness can make us more resilient and creative, harder working, healthier and even help us to live longer. Are you convinced?

2. Watch a 20-minute online lecture given by Carl Honore, based on his book *In Praise of Slow*, attacking the 'cult of speed': www.youtube.com/watch?v=UhXiHJ8vfuk

Then consider:
- To what extent is modern life trapped in a culture of speed?
- What might be the value of a slower approach to life?
- What are the implications of this for educational practice?

Author's note

My personal and professional interest in wellbeing has developed considerably over the past three years. This stems partly from visiting India with mature students a couple of times and following a course called 'Gandhi and Globalization' led by three prominent Gandhian scholars, including Satish Kumar (see earlier references). The trips have also involved visiting local schools and observing at close hand the everyday lives of Indian citizens and children. I have been struck by the dramatic impact of these experiences on my own values and attitudes as well as those of many of the mature students on these visits. I have seen remarkable transformations in the outlooks of mature and experienced teachers in their forties and fifties over just a few weeks, all of which suggests that powerful emotional and psychological processes of change have been set in train through this direct experience.

I have subsequently reflected upon my own personal and professional life and redirected much of my energy into activities I believe to be more worthwhile and wellbeing related. This has included reading around the extensive literature on wellbeing and happiness, which has been immensely stimulating and has also resulted in the development of a new module on wellbeing for the BA (Hons) degree which I am involved in at the University of Plymouth. After some twenty-eight years of involvement in education at secondary school, further education and presently HE, I am now convinced that here is one of the most significant and worthwhile developments I have run into and I hope the reader will be sufficiently stimulated by this chapter to want to explore their professional practice and the growing literature further.

Further reading

De Graaf, J., Wann, D. and Naylor, T. (2005), *Affluenza*. San Francisco: Berrett-Koehler.

Layard, R. (2005), *Happiness: lessons from a new science*. London: Penguin.

Noddings, N. (2003), *Happiness and Education*. New York: Cambridge University Press.

References

Ben-Shahar, T. (2006), 'Make lemonade out of lemons', *Guardian*, 25 April.

Brighouse, H. (2006), *On Education: Thinking in Action*. London and New York: Routledge.

Brookfield, S. (2006), *The Power of Critical Theory for Adult Learning and Teaching*. Maidenhead: Open University Press.

Craig, C. (2007), *The Potential Dangers of a Systematic, Explicit Approach to Teaching Social and Emotional Skills (SEAL)*. Glasgow: Centre for Confidence and Wellbeing.

Daily Telegraph (2007), 'In full: Cameron's speech on childhood', *Daily Telegraph*, 27 March.

De Graaf, J., Wann, D. and Naylor, T. (2005), *Affluenza*. San Francisco: Berrett-Koehler.

Department for Education and Skills (2007), 'Social and emotional aspects of learning'. www.standards.dfes.gov.uk/primary/publications/banda/seal/ (accessed 10 December 2007).

Ecclestone, K. (2007), 'All in the mind', *Guardian*, 27 February.

Furedi, F. (2003), *Therapy Culture*. London: Routledge.

Goleman, D. (1996), *Emotional Intelligence*. London: Bloomsbury.

Goodley, D. (2007), 'For inclusion: towards a critical pedagogy with marginalised learners'. www.leeds.ac.uk/disability-studies/archiveuk/goodley/inclusive%20pedagogy.pdf (accessed 21 November 2007).

Haidt, J. (2006), *The Happiness Hypothesis*. London: Arrow.

Hawn Foundation (2007). www.thehawnfoundation.org/ (accessed 21 November 2007).

Hird, S. (2003), *What is Wellbeing? A Brief Review of Current Literature and Concepts*. NHS Health Scotland.

Honore, C. (2004), *In Praise of Slow*. London: Orion.

Huppert, F., Baylis, N. and Keverne, B. (eds) (2005), *The Science of Well-being*. Oxford: Oxford University Press.

Inglehart, R. (1971), 'The silent revolution in post-industrial societies', *American Political Science Review*, 65, 991–1017.

James, O. (1998), *Britain on the Couch*. London: Arrow.

Kasser, T. (2002), *The High Price of Materialism*. London: MIT Press.

Kasser, T. and Kanner, A. (2004), *Psychology and Consumer Culture*. Washington, DC: American Psychological Association.

Kumar, S. (2004), *No Destination*. Totnes: Resurgence.

Layard, R. (2005), *Happiness: lessons from a new science*. London: Penguin.

Layard, R. (2007), *Happiness and the Teaching of Values*. Centrepiece: Summer.

Midlands Psychology Group (2007), 'Questioning the science and politics of happiness', *The Psychologist*, 20(7), 422–425.

Newton, J. (2007), 'Wellbeing: Contributions towards practical strategies to promote social integration'. Paper presented at UN expert meeting on Creating and Inclusive Society: Practical Strategies to Promote Social Integration. Paris, France, 10–13 September 2007.

Noddings, N. (2005), *Happiness and Education*. New York: Cambridge University Press.

NPR (2007), 'Going bowling'. www.npr.org/templates/story/story.php?storyId=1074874 (accessed 27 November 2007).

Oswald, A. (2007), 'Affluenza: a review'. www2.warwick.ac.uk/fac/soc/economics/staff/faculty/oswald/affluenzajan07.pdf (accessed 12 December 2007).

Putnam, R. (2000), *Bowling Alone*. New York: Simon & Schuster.

Schoch, R. (2007), *The Secrets of Happiness*. London: Profile Books.

Seligman, M.E.P., Steen, T.A., Park, N. and Peterson, C. (2005), 'Positive psychology progress: empirical validation of interventions', *American Psychologist*, 60(5), 410–421.

Sumedho, A. (2007), 'Buddhist psychology, getting real about the human condition'. Paper presented at Happiness and Its Causes conference. London: Terrapin.

UNICEF (2007), 'Child poverty in perspective: An overview of child well-being in rich countries'. *Innocenti Report Card 7*, UNICEF Innocenti Research Centre: Florence.

Wellington College (2007), '"Happiness" lessons start at Wellington'. www.wellington-college.berks.sch.uk/page.aspx?id=595 (accessed 21 November 2007).

Where should Pupils who Experience Social, Emotional and Behavioural Difficulties (SEBD) be Educated?

Helen Knowler

Chapter Outline

Where do I belong?   106
Words matter   107
The historic 'burden' of SEBD   108
Including pupils who experience SEBD   110
Mainstream school or special school:
does it really matter where pupils are taught?   111
Belonging and school   113
Conclusion   114
Author's note   115

[T]he concept of inclusion must embrace the feeling of belonging, since such a feeling appears to be necessary for successful learning and for more general wellbeing.

(Warnock, 2005: 15)

Can you ever remember a time when you did not belong? Can you remember the depth of emotion that this feeling evoked? Perhaps it was a temporary feeling associated with a time when you attended a new school or the time you moved into secondary school. Perhaps you joined a club to take up a new hobby, but very soon you realized that this was not for you – you did not belong.

For a lot of people 'belonging' is something they take for granted. We belong in our families, in our network of friends and in our learning communities. For some people the feeling that they do not belong is a serious threat to their inclusion and participation in education and in society. Pupils described as having Social, Emotional and Behavioural Difficulties (SEBD) have been identified as a group who are least likely to receive effective support in school and the most likely to receive support too late (Ofsted, 2006). The personal, social and educational outcomes for this group of pupils is the poorest of all groups with SEN and it is fair to say, from the evidence presented in numerous research accounts, that for these pupils the experience of inclusion has not been a good one. Frederickson and collegues (2007) found that, on the whole, pupils with SEN have lower social status and are more likely to be rejected by their peers because of their difference, and less well integrated because of the disruption they cause to the learning of others. Harris and colleagues (2006) suggest that the high numbers of pupils who are currently either excluded from school or disaffected and at serious risk of permanent exclusion is evidence that the inclusion agenda is seriously challenged by pupils who find school a difficult place to be. Many studies conclude that, of all the groups of children and young people who have been included in mainstream provision during the last twenty years – for example, those with sensory impairments or specific learning difficulties such as dyslexia – SEBD is the hardest to accommodate (Davis and Florian, 2004; Head and Pirrie, 2007; Ofsted, 2005, 2006; Wise, 1999). In this chapter I argue that one of the reasons these pupils have not experienced inclusion in a positive way is because of the way their inclusion is seen in terms of *where* they are educated rather than *how* they are educated – and that fundamentally the school system to which they are subjected very often fails to foster the sense of belonging essential for developing transformative inclusionary experiences.

In the first section of this chapter I ask 'Where do I belong?' in order to outline my own position on the issue of belonging and SEBD. In order to clarify what we understand by the term SEBD, I then explore definitions of the term and discuss the 'burden' that this label implies (Clough et al., 2005). I argue that inclusion for pupils identified as having SEBD is different to that for other groups of learners and some teachers fail to recognize what could be described as creative and innovative practice for supporting this group. In my experience, inclusion in some mainstream settings refers to things being the same: the same classroom, the same lesson content, the same curricular areas, the same assessment practices and the same learning outcomes. This could be because of a model of inclusion that teachers recognize from their own experience of professional development or because that is the way that schools understand inclusion. The systems put in place to support pupils seem to be more for the benefit of the school than out of responsiveness to individual need; for example, the need for calm and order (Thomas, 2005). In the final section of the chapter I suggest that, in the case of pupils who are identified as having SEBD, it might be more useful to consider the concept of belonging as a prerequisite to successful inclusion. Fostering a feeling of belonging can be done wherever a pupil is educated, and so rather than engaging in unhelpful debates about whether it is best that pupils are in mainstream schools or special schools, I present my own research findings that indicate that mainstream schools and special schools have the capacity to offer pupils what they need to be included and that 'effective provision' can be developed anywhere.

Where do I belong?

Having outlined what I will explore in this chapter it is useful to highlight the why. Two overarching themes will emerge and, although presented separately here, they are inter-related. These themes run throughout the chapter and so rather than reading this as repetition, it should be recognized as evidence of the pervasiveness of these issues in the field of SEBD (Burman, 2003).

I contend that the discourse of school effectiveness over the last ten years is in direct conflict with what research says about effective practice for pupils with SEBD. The high status that is given to academic outcomes and the production of league tables has made it much harder for schools to show progress for these individuals. The 'value' of pupils who are unlikely to gain academic qualifications (in the wrong environment), and indeed may even jeopardize the academic outcomes for others, makes them an undesirable addition to some school communities. Verkuyten (2002) argues that evaluative judgements about classroom behaviour place teachers in accountable positions – if you cannot control your class what does this say about you as a teacher? What will others thinks as they observe your poor classroom control? These are further reasons why pupils with challenging behaviour are not always welcomed.

Frederickson and colleagues (2007) note that outcomes in education are rarely measured in terms of the impact upon personal or social development of an individual – so that the notion of 'educational outcomes' is actually about academic evidence of attainment rather than a reflection of total achievements of an individual throughout their school career. This relates directly to the theme of belonging, since if as an individual what you have to offer the school community is perceived to be neither valuable nor desirable, your sense of belonging within that community is likely to be diminished. The sense of belonging/not belonging is also a theme in Hannah Smith's discussion of Deaf Culture in Chapter 4.

Belonging is a significant challenge for pupils identified as having SEBD and this is related to the second theme to run throughout the chapter – that of location. If you feel you belong, you are more likely to be included, to feel included and therefore to participate. However, pupils in this group often find themselves in a number of different placements throughout their school career, ranging from mainstream provision, to Pupil Referral Units (PRUs) to 365 days per year residential care environments. Feelings of belonging are therefore much harder to support and sustain.

Belonging has long been seen as a significant consideration in education, in theory (Glasser, 1986; Maslow, 1970), and in research that suggests there is a link between feelings of belonging and increased levels of motivation, engagement with learning, greater willingness to participate and reduction in disruptive incidents in the classroom (Audit Commission, 2002; Booth and Ainscow, 2002; Frederickson et al., 2007). However, because the issue of inclusion for pupils with SEBD appears to centre around *where* they should be taught, the issue of *what* they should be taught and *how* seems to have become the less prominent concern. My own research (Knowler and Waite, 2006) has highlighted that many of the things are identified as 'good practice' within special schools are not the exclusive remit of special education and, in agreement with Visser (2005), I believe that there are many things that any school can do to support inclusion that do not depend upon the building in which they take place. If teachers do not feel that the pupils in their classes should be there because they perceive that they do not have the capacity to support such a placement, it is unlikely that feelings of belonging with be nurtured as part of the provision for that individual.

Words matter

What we call people who find school a difficult place to be matters a great deal. The language we use to describe or label pupils has implications for the way we plan provision and support for them. What we call pupils impacts upon the way they are talked about in staffrooms, the way that they are treated by peers and the way that they are provided for by Local Authorities when assessing statements of special educational needs. O'Brien (2005) asserts that by describing a pupil as 'having SEBD' or 'with SEBD' we suggest that the problem lies within the individual. If a pupil 'has' SEBD, it tends to suggest that it is a permanent state that is fixed – like a medical condition. It tends to suggest that the individual is in a constant state of turmoil and that their social, emotional and behavioural development is impaired. This is not always necessarily the case, but from this set of assumptions the teacher is positioned as 'helper' (Thomas, 2005). The problem is clearly with the individual. It highlights difference in a way that tends to suggest 'you have a problem and therefore you don't belong here'.

However, if we conceptualize the notion of SEBD as something that an individual *experiences*, we begin to see the issue of including pupils in a very different light. To say that a pupil *experiences* SEBD infers that this is something that happens in particular circumstances and as a result of contextual influences, rather than a condition that exists *within* the child or young person. When we think about SEBD as something that is *experienced* by an individual, it seems to better explain what we observe going on in classrooms – that is, pupils do not experience difficulties in every subject area, with every teacher they work with or in every school they are placed. For the remainder of this chapter I will refer to individuals as those who *experience* SEBD, concurring with O'Brien's (2005) view that learners experience SEBD because they 'find themselves in situations that they perceive as intolerable'.

The historic 'burden' of SEBD

Clough and colleagues (2005) say that SEBD carries a 'burden' that other areas of Special Educational Needs (SEN) do not. The themes that emerge from a variety of other literature suggest this 'burden' might be constituted by a lack of consensus in definitions, a lack of resources to support individuals, the individualistic nature of the associated problems with SEBD, a lack of literature regarding pedagogy (O'Brien, 2005), or the social implications such as anti-social behaviour and crime.

SEBD have been called many different things throughout the last 100 years. They are not new and have remained a concern for schools and teachers despite the implementation of policy initiatives and government strategies to try to 'eliminate' behaviour problems in our schools (DfES, 1989). The link between behaviour in schools and anti-social behaviour and crime has made the drive for quick solutions and answers to complex problems pressing for governments. There appears to be a belief that by tackling problem behaviour in schools the ills of society will be vanquished. The drive towards the publication of league tables to measure the 'performance' of schools has rendered SEBD an even more undesirable problem for many schools. Children who experience SEBD get in the way of achieving high grades – their 'worth' in terms of their ability to gain academic qualifications is low and therefore interventions that might support improved educational attainment are experienced as a costly resource in terms of time, money, staff and upon the reputation of the school.

There have been a variety of terms to describe children who experience SEBD, such as 'maladjusted', 'disturbed' or suffering a 'conduct disorder'. Cole (2005) reports that in the nineteenth century children who displayed challenging behaviour were described as 'mental defectives' or 'moral imbeciles'. In the early part of the twentieth century, as education began to address issues regarding the fundamental nature of schooling, the focus was very much upon diagnosis and treatment, following a medical model of intervention. A child's fitness for the classroom was assessed and those deemed to be too 'disturbed' were placed in special provision. Treatment focused upon psychiatric and psychoanalytic interventions designed to find the 'cause' within the child, usually believed to be a result of some trauma or 'damage' to the child in early infancy. Children often attended 'schools for the maladjusted' and were kept away from the mainstream population. Internationally the definitions for SEBD also 'gloss' over the complex issues of provision (Winzer, 2005) so that terminology differs across national boundaries – in Israel 'mentally disturbed', in Poland 'socially maladjusted' and in Slovakia 'defective behaviour'.

The Elton Report (DfES, 1989) was at the time the most comprehensive review of discipline in schools and was a key document in highlighting educational questions in supporting children in schools who experience SEBD. It investigated dimensions such as teaching and learning, schools structures, links with the community, the role of parents and outside agencies. Elton encouraged schools to focus upon aspects of teachers' practice such as the 'pace' of teaching, the type of topics taught, the importance of explicit 'boundary setting' by adults and personal relationships with pupils, as means to establishing effective provision. The poor educational outcomes of pupils who did not behave in schools were noted and, despite a raft of recommendations, many were largely ignored – this may be due in some part to the simultaneous introduction of the National Curriculum. One could reasonably assume that this became a major priority for teachers who were working in schools in 1989.

By the time the revised National Curriculum was introduced in 2000, containing a clear statement consistent with the development of inclusive philosophy throughout the late 1990s, schools were grappling with the strong message in education policy that children with SEBD should first and foremost attend mainstream provision, unless there was a very good reason why they should not or their parents wished them to attend specialist provision. *Removing Barriers to Achievement* (DfES, 2004) made it explicit that the teacher was responsible for removing potential barriers to the inclusion of children with SEN such as access to the curriculum, assessment opportunities, identifying learning difficulties and differentiating classroom tasks and pedagogy appropriately.

School improvement literature is beginning to take account of the social and emotional dimensions of learning and to recognize the significance of belonging to a school community as an important building block for inclusion (Goleman, 1996; Weare, 2000, 2004). (Tony Brown's chapter in this collection offers insights into the relational nature of learning.) Policy initiatives such as the Social and Emotional Aspects of Learning (SEAL) materials (DfES, 2005) provide a clear framework to help schools develop structures that build supportive cultures.

Including pupils who experience SEBD

Lines (2003) suggests that responding to challenging behaviour is a complex task. O'Brien (2005) concurs and argues that, despite this, many schools are searching for easy 'quick fix' solutions to complex problems – solutions that are more likely to be designed to reduce stress levels experienced by the adults in schools. Head and Pirrie (2007) prompt us to think about the most appropriate provision for pupils who have failed to meet the challenges that attending mainstream schools have presented. Conversely, I would challenge readers to think about what can be done about the way that mainstream schools have failed to respond to the challenges that pupils who experience SEBD have presented to mainstream school structures.

The concept of inclusion remains complex and confused for many teachers, who believe that if a child who experiences SEBD is *in* the classroom, you are, by default, working in an inclusive way. Schools rarely plan and deliver interventions designed for individuals, preferring to subject children with difficulties to the loosely based and often ill-thought-out behaviour policy that was previously gathering dust on the shelf in the headteacher's office – and not one that has been developed with supporting a particular individual in mind. Provision for including pupils with SEBD needs to take account of the social and emotional aspects of learning first and foremost, because without the support in these areas it is unlikely that learning will take place anyway.

Mainstream school or special school: does it really matter where pupils are taught?

Daniels and Cole (2002) remind us that children and young people who experience SEBD form part of a group whose needs are often in direct conflict with the needs of a much larger group (usually a class of thirty others). In mainstream schools they will usually be placed in much larger groups, where it is harder for individuals to feel that they are receiving the attention that is needed to build positive relationships and self-esteem. The building of positive relationships is noted as a crucial factor across a wide range of literature, and while some of this research suggests that individuals who experience SEBD are railing against the school system, Solomon and Rogers (2001) say that there will be some individuals who will be unable to meet the requirements of the mainstream school environment regardless of factors such as curriculum, teachers, environment, additional support and teaching time. What this illustrates is that the educational response for some individuals (e.g., stick to the rules and do more work) is inappropriate and what they do not need is the pressure to further conform to the notion of an 'ideal' pupil. Interestingly Solomon and Rogers (2001) found that pupils who experience SEBD often enjoyed an egalitarian relationship with the teacher, with an emphasis on what they called an 'apprenticeship-style' approach to learning. If this is the case more generally, then there are implications for the way that teaching and learning is organized for this particular group of pupils.

Mainstream schools offer provision where pupils can be educated alongside their peers, where difference and diversity can be celebrated. Jenkinson (1997) suggests that the existence of special schools should not suggest that a different system of education is available, but in my experience that is exactly what teachers in mainstream schools, struggling to support a pupil experiencing SEBD, think. There appears to be a perception that the only place pupils with SEBD can be educated is in special schools. This idea is likely to be influenced by the existence in special schools of smaller class sizes, greater perceived teacher expertise, more resources, and opportunities for multi-agency working and the use of therapeutic services to support pupils. Mainstream positions itself in deficit – with neither the resources nor expertise to teach pupils who experience SEBD. However, instead of seeing the two types of provision as separate, I would argue that it is better to view mainstream schools and special schools as part of a continuum of provision available for pupils who experience SEBD. There is an assumption made in some schools that if a pupil fails to cope in a particular mainstream school, then they probably need to be in a special school. However, knowing that behaviour problems are highly contextual and responsive to localized conditions, pupils may thrive in a different mainstream school (see Harris et al., 2006 for a further explanation of the concept of managed moves). However, should the second mainstream school offer more or less the same provision in terms of teaching support, curriculum content, assessment, approaches to timetabling, then it is likely the pupil will once again be excluded. My own research has led me to conclude that special schools do indeed offer something that supports positive outcomes for pupils who experience SEBD – but my question remains as to whether these things are entirely the remit of special schools or whether these ways of working can be incorporated into mainstream systems. Table 7.1 provides a brief outline of the factors pupils said made a difference to their education. The pupils I worked with were educated in special residential provision, many of them having been excluded from a number of mainstream and special school placements.

It is hard to envisage how any of the areas identified by the youngsters taking part in the research could not be developed equally well by a mainstream setting or a special setting.

However, problems with placements are not unique to mainstream schools. The difficulties of matching provision to individual needs is well documented (Visser et al., 2005; Ofsted, 2006; Farrell and Polat, 2003). The continuing problem of special school provision deemed to be unsatisfactory by government inspectors has exacerbated an already complex issue (Ofsted, 2006),

Table 7.1 Summary of factors that pupils consider to make a difference to their education (Knowler and Waite, 2006)

Pupils need to be perceived as *individuals*	A 'one-size-fits-all' approach is to be avoided as far as possible. There is no blueprint for effective provision and it should not be assumed that what works for one pupil would automatically work for another.
Opportunities for *genuine participation*	Moving beyond the tokenistic, pupils have a say in what happens to them and their views are considered when planning interventions or strategies to support them.
Expertise, humour and warmth	We assume that since none of the participants mentioned behaviour management skills in staff, that these were so well embedded that what pupils actually noticed was expertise, humour and warmth.
Excellent communication	This was assumed because pupils said that the people they worked with understood them. It is vital that staff understand the social, emotional and educational needs of the individuals they work with.
Consistency	A key element that appeared to make a difference and this did not just mean in terms of 'behaviour sanctions' or 'rules'. Pupils talked about people meaning what they said and always following through, they mentioned the fact that there was a key person in whom they could trust. It appears that services within placements (e.g., education and care) were given equal status, that is one was no more crucial than the other in the support they gave.

which calls into question the evidence that special schools are necessarily the most appropriate place for pupils to be educated.

Belonging and school

Visser and colleagues (2005) remind us that 'missing' children who experience SEBD (i.e. pupils who are excluded from mainstream and no longer attend alternative provision) have chosen not to engage in what education, school in particular, can offer. They suggest that these children and young people may see school as 'irrelevant to their aspirations; experiencing teaching and learning at an inappropriate level' (ibid.: 45). Farrell and Polat (2003) ask whether mainstream provision could ever offer the care and support needed by pupils who experience SEBD to help them overcome their emotional and behavioural problems. It is clear that whether provision in mainstream, special or something else, if it has been designed to meet the needs of the individual it can help individuals to overcome difficulties, increase their opportunities for participation and achieve. Well-planned and appropriate placements have the potential to make a difference to the lives of pupils who experience SEBD.

As a result of her research Reed (2005) suggests that things that contribute to the success of inclusion in particular setting are actually about wider factors such as the school culture and practice of individual teachers, suggesting that where the inclusion and participation of pupils experiencing behaviour problems is a priority for the schools, there are more positive outcomes for all concerned.

The educational and social outcomes for pupils who experience SEBD are poor (Ofsted, 2006). The question of how they are educated is crucial in ensuring that not only do they have the opportunity to grow to be adults who can fulfil the outcomes of the Every Child Matters agenda (DfES, 2003) but also that their needs are fully recognized and met while they are in school, rather than being considered once they are excluded from full-time education.

Conclusion

There continue to be major challenges to the successful inclusion of pupils who experience SEBD. I have argued in this chapter that a debate about where they are educated belies the complexity of the problem. I have argued that until school communities recognize that inclusion for pupils who experience SEBD is linked to their feelings of belonging, the dichotomized nature of the debate about special and mainstream schools will be a 'red herring' that ultimately does little to increase opportunities for participation for this group of pupils. A *range* of suitable provision (i.e. mainstream *and* special) that has the capacity to meet the needs of an individual is to be welcomed and desired. The danger of placing pupils in provision which is not suitable for them academically, personally and socially remains a real threat to the inclusion agenda. The issue of location will continue to perpetuate exclusionary practices that enable the removal of children and young people from school communities – in the hope that by putting them somewhere else we are solving a problem (Lines, 2003).

For critical reflection

- What do you understand by the term *Social, Emotional and Behavioural Difficulties*? Critically reflect upon your own attitudes, values and beliefs about this area of SEN and the implications for appropriate provision.

⇨

- Consider effective provision for pupils who experience SEBD. What are the opportunities and limitations of provision that is organized in mainstream schools?
- Critically reflect upon assessment procedures that are currently adopted in many schools. Consider practices that foster a sense of belonging and those that may be described as exclusionary.
- Consider models of professional development for teachers and reflect upon the impact of these models in building the capacity of teachers to support pupils with challenging and difficult behaviour.

Author's note

My interest in children who experience SEBD was borne out of necessity. My first teaching post was in a Year 6 class in a school in Sandwell in the West Midlands. Some children displayed challenging behaviour and some did not. The ones that did, swore, walked out of lessons, answered back and called one rude names under their breath. One dealt with it and got on with it like all the other teachers in the school. I think that I worked out fairly quickly that while these behaviours appeared to be blatant threats to teacher authority, it would do me little good to enter into confrontations. I would probably lose. However, this led me to consider my own behaviour, teaching and classroom organization. I can remember making a concerted effort to make what I did relevant, interesting and involving the children in decisions about topics, activities and assessment. I also thought that positive relationships were important and that if you hated school you would probably misbehave. So I made building positive relationships a priority and I think that I had some success. I felt smug enough to think I was good at it and thought if one had worked in schools such as this, one can work anywhere. I was wrong.

When I moved to Devon I had no idea that my so-called 'skills' in this area would be stretched to the limit, and even rendered useless. I had a Year 5 class that had twenty-nine 'good' children and one child with a statement of Special Educational Needs (SEN) for SEBD. This evolved into a very difficult year, and for me made a distinction between teaching in a particular location where the pupils are perceived as 'tough' and teaching a pupil who is experiencing SEBD within a class of those who do not. The problem for me was that I thought I *had* developed skills, knowledge and experience that I assumed would be applicable wherever I happened to teach – and this was not the case. This is where my real interest in this area of SEN began to develop. I began to ask myself questions regarding the nature of the knowledge I needed in order to teach pupils who experience SEBD in mainstream settings. I wondered how I could overcome some of the inherent tensions in a mainstream setting when trying to include children with complex and challenging behaviour, such as the National Curriculum, assessment procedures, class size and generic behaviour policies which adopt 'one-size-fits-all' approaches. It was also around this time that I began to notice the way that the issue of SEBD in mainstream created emotive and strong opinions about the viability of including children in mainstream classrooms. There did not appear to be much fence-sitting! Teachers I talked to either believed that all children had a right to a broad and balanced curriculum with their peers, and that it was the teacher's job to find a way to make it work, or believed the complete opposite, that is, these children spoil the education of others and should be placed in a separate special provision. The Ofsted (2006) report *Inclusion: Does it Matter Where Pupils are Taught?* makes reference to the fact that while other groups of pupils with SEN experience many beneficial advantages by attending mainstream schools, those who are identified as 'having' SEBD are still the most difficult to accommodate. This wasn't the first document I had read to say it and probably will not be the last.

I continued to be fascinated by the role of the teacher in the successful inclusion of children who experience SEBD in mainstream settings. I have, over the years, considered a variety of factors that affect the way a teacher works with pupils with behaviour problems, such as school culture, the headteacher, values and beliefs, knowledge and skills, the management of stress, policy and procedure, curriculum organization and staff 'training'. I have seen some practitioners who work with this group of pupils very successfully and I have seen people who do not. I have been on countless training courses and delivered countless training courses and observed that in many cases this has had little impact on the practice of some teachers, in terms of perceived positive educational outcomes for children. This area continues to fascinate me and I still enjoy going into schools and working with teachers to develop innovative and creative ways of supporting vulnerable pupils.

Further reading

Clough, P., Garner, P., Pardeck, J. and Yuen, F. (eds), (2005), *Handbook of Social Emotional and Behavioural Difficulties*. London: Sage.

O'Brien, T. (2005), 'Social, emotional behavioural difficulties', in A. Lewis and B. Norwich (eds), (2005), *Special Teaching for Special Children: Pedagogies for Inclusion*. Maidenhead: Open University Press.

Thomas, G. and Loxley, A. (2001), *Deconstructing Special Education*. Maidenhead: Open University Press.

References

Audit Commission (2002), *Special Educational Needs: A Mainstream Issue*. London: Audit Commission.

Booth, T. and Ainscow, M. (2002), *Index for Inclusion: Developing Learning and Participation in School*. Bristol: CSIE.

Burman, E. (2003), *Deconstucting Developmental Psychology*. London: Routledge.

Clough, P., Garner, P., Pardeck, J. and Yuen, F. (eds), (2005), *Handbook of Emotional and Behavioural Difficulties*. London: Sage.

Cole, T. (2005), 'Emotional and behavioural difficulties: an historical perspective', in P. Clough, P. Garner, J. Pardeck and F. Yuen (eds), *Handbook of Emotional and Behavioural Difficulties*. London: Sage.

Daniel, H. and Cole, T. (2002), 'The development of provision for young people with emotional and behavioural difficulties: an activity theory analysis', *Oxford Review of Education*, 28(2 and 3), 311–329.

Davis, P. and Florian, L. (2004), *Teaching Strategies and Approaches for Pupils with Special Educational Needs: A Scoping Study*. Norwich: DfES.

DfES (1989), *Discipline in Schools: Report of the Committee of Enquired Chaired by Lord Elton*. London: HMSO.

Department for Education and Skills (DfES) (2003), *Every Child Matters: Green Paper*. London: The Stationery Office.

DfES (2004), *Removing Barriers to Achievement*. London: DfES.

DfES (2005), *Excellence and Enjoyment: The Social and Emotional Aspects of Learning*. Nottingham: DfES.

Farrell, P. and Polat, F. (2003), 'The long-term impact of residential provision for pupils with emotional and behavioural difficulties', *European Journal of Special Educational Needs*, 18(3), 277–292.

Frederickson, N., Simmonds, E., Evans, L. and Soulsby, C. (2007), 'Assessing the social and affective outcomes of inclusion', *British Journal of Special Education*, 34(2), 105–115.

Glasser, W. (1986), *Control Theory in the Classroom*. New York: Harper and Row.

Goleman, D. (1996), *Emotional Intelligence*. London: Bloomsbury.

Harris, B., Vincent, K., Thomson, P. and Toalster, R. (2006), 'Does every child know they matter? Pupils' views of one alternative to exclusion', *Pastoral Care in Education*, June, 28–38.

Head, G. and Pirrie, A. (2007), 'The place of special schools in a policy climate of inclusion', *Journal of Research in Special Educational Needs*, 7(2), 90–96.

Jenkinson, J. (1997), *Mainstream or Special: Educating Students with Disabilities*. London: Routledge.

Knowler, H. and Waite, S. (2006), 'Factors that pupils with behaviour, emotional and social difficulties (BESD) consider make a difference to their education in Dorset's out of county residential (OCR) or Local Authority (LA) provision'. Plymouth: University of Plymouth, unpublished report.

Lines, D. (2003), 'Insights into the management of challenging behaviour in school', *Pastoral Care in Education*, March, 26–36.

Maslow, A. (1970), *Motivation and Personality*. New York: Harper and Row.

O'Brien, T. (2005), 'Social, emotional behavioural difficulties', in A. Lewis and B. Norwich (eds), *Special Teaching for Special Children: Pedagogies for Inclusion*. Maidenhead: Open University Press.

Ofsted (2005), *Inclusion: The Impact of LEA Support and Outreach Services* (No. HMI 2452). London: HMI.

Ofsted (2006), *Inclusion: Does it Matter Where Pupils are Taught? Provision and Outcomes in Different Settings for Pupils with Learning Difficulties*. London: HMI.

Reed, J. (2005), *Classroom Lessons for Policy Makers: Toward Zero Exclusion Project.* London: Institute for Public Policy Research (IPPR).

Solomon, Y. and Rogers, C. (2001), 'Motivational patterns in disaffected school students: insights from pupil referral unit clients', *British Educational Research Journal,* 27(3), 331–345.

Thomas, G. (2005), 'What do we mean by EBD?', in P. Clough, P. Garner, J. Pardeck and F. Yuen (eds), *Handbook of Emotional Behavioural Difficulties.* London: Sage.

Verkuyten, M. (2002), 'Making teachers accountable for students' disruptive classroom behaviour', *British Journal of Sociology of Education,* 23(1), 107–122.

Visser, J. (2005), 'Working with children and young people with social, emotional and behavioural difficulties: what makes what works, work?', in P. Clough, P. Garner, J. Pardeck and F. Yuen (eds), *Handbook of Emotional and Behavioural Difficulties.* London: Sage.

Visser, J., Daniels, H. and MacNab, N. (2005), 'Missing: children and young people with SEBD', *Emotional and Behavioural Difficulties,* 10(1), 43–54.

Warnock, M. (2005), *Special Educational Needs: A New Outlook.* London: Philosophy of Education Society of Great Britain.

Weare, K. (2000), *Promoting Mental, Emotional and Social Health.* London: Routledge.

Weare, K. (2004), *Developing the Emotionally Literate School.* London: Paul Chapman.

Winzer, M. (2005), 'International comparisons in EBD: critical issues', in P. Clough, P. Garner, J. Pardeck and F. Yuen (eds), *Handbook of Emotional and Behavourial Difficulties.* London: Sage.

Wise, S. (1999), 'Improving success in the mainstream settings for pupils with emotional and behavioural difficulties', *Pastoral Care in Education,* September, 14–20.

Part Three
Approaches to Participation

Informal Learning Outdoors
Tony Rea

Chapter Outline

The nature of informal learning	122
Participation in informal learning outdoors: benefits and learner outcomes	125
Current debates about challenge and risk in the outdoors and how this might affect participation	126
A pedagogy for outdoor learning?	127
Author's note	131

This chapter considers the range and breadth of outdoor learning opportunities and how these relate to the inclusion agenda, and engages positively with current debates about challenge and risk in the outdoors. As the introduction to the book suggests, there is a discrepancy in education between the agenda of 'pupil participation' and 'inclusive education' stated in policy documents (government, school, outdoor education centre) and a reality of exclusivity.

Questions of who is 'in' and who is left 'out' are complex in outdoor settings. The Duke of Edinburgh Award Scheme has been used to extend 'gifted and talented' pupils in some schools, and in others as an alternative curriculum for 'under achievers'. Forest schools are sometimes provided as a treat for the 'disengaged' to be quickly removed should they misbehave, and at other times as an entitlement for the very youngest pre-schools and nurseries. There are many examples of outdoor activities being used to re-engage 'reluctant learners' or those with 'challenging behaviour' in outdoor centres and pupil referral units. Many of these terms – gifted, talented, underachievers, disengaged, reluctant learners, challenging behaviour – are situated within discourses of exclusivity or self/other, and this chapter challenges these discourses, arguing that outdoor learning is for everyone.

In this chapter I question the oft-claimed link between outdoor learning and improved academic achievement and self-esteem. Uncritically accepting such claims arguably contains the danger that outdoor education will become increasingly like traditional schooling and thus affected by the same inclusion/participation issues that surround schooling. This is explored further in case study 1.

The nature of informal learning

As humans we are built to learn, and do so easily. Much, if not most, of what we know and can do has been learnt informally, out of school. Schooling is a modern phenomenon that has been widespread in most developed countries for about 150 years. It was not common before the early nineteenth century, is not universally accepted and may not last the test of time. The differences between informal learning and schooling as shown in Table 8.1 have been discussed by Desforges (1995) and Kelly (2007).

I see the consideration of informal learning outdoors as central to a broadened concept of inclusion. 'Outdoor learning' is a problematic term, one that needs defining. Stables (2005) sees 'learning' as a reified theoretical concept and prefers the term 'making meaning from experience' as a more useful, descriptive term. In my use of the term 'outdoor learning', I use learning as a metaphor for 'constructing meaning from experience'. So, I consider learning as something that *happens* when people interact with each other in a social context, and/or with the environment. Thus, I am adopting a social–constructivist view of learning, which is based on the philosophical position that knowledge does not exist outside of human and social discourses.

Table 8.1 Informal learning and schooling

Informal learning	Schooling
Led by learner interest and enthusiasm	Led by curriculum design and national orthodoxies, such as 'intended learning outcomes' defined by teachers
An imperative to know, or be able to do, something	An imperative to test
At the pace of the learners, at a time and in a place determined by them	Controlled by semesters, academic terms, timetables and over-structured lesson designs

The outdoors can provide opportunities for far richer experiences from which to construct meaning than do classrooms and schools (Hattie et al., 1997). Why this may be so is not easy to determine. It may be because of the place, the activity carried out in the place or a person's affinity to the place, or more likely a combination of these factors. Defining the outdoors can also be difficult. Whilst some contexts are unproblematic – for example, a moor, mountain, forest – others are problematic. For example, is a cave inside or outside? If I am snuggled in my berth, in a cabin of a small boat being tossed around on a big sea, am I inside or outdoors? I once wrote a short case study based on powerful learning experiences that took place in a lambing shed on a Somerset farm (Rea and Waite, 2007). I called this outdoor learning, but was it? Similarly, some of the activities associated with the outdoors can be accomplished indoors; for example, climbing and canoeing.

I have taken a broad view of what constitutes the outdoors, central to which is a distancing from schools and schooling, and the formality that often accompanies these. I prefer outdoor 'learning' to outdoor 'education'. Learning is a less formal and more inclusive term that values everything learned, not just learning which matches someone else's professional definition or meets certain pre-designed objectives.

The range and breadth of outdoor learning opportunities is vast. Rickinson and colleagues (2004) have divided opportunities into headings, three of which are used in Table 8.2. They have been written about elsewhere (Re'em, 2001) and some of the theory used to explain their effectiveness overlaps with what I introduce below.

In the past, participation in many of the activities in Table 8.2, especially those in the centre column, was almost exclusively for the socially privileged.

Table 8.2 Opportunities for participation in learning outdoors

Field studies and visits	Adventurous activities	School grounds
Farm visits	Outdoor centres	Planting and growing
Forest schools	Rock climbing	Orienteering
Geography studies	Canoeing	Outdoor art
Scientific studies	Caving	Outdoor drama
	Walking	Wide games, 'ride-on' toys, sand
	Expeditions	and water play, climbing equipment
	Ten Tors Challenge	
	Sailing, sail training	
	Riding	
	Camping	
	Scouting and guiding	

This position began to change during the twentieth century. The Scout Movement (Baden-Powell, 1930) has long thrived in under-privileged areas, the Duke of Edinburgh's Award Scheme is an example of how participation in such activities has been made more affordable to many, and much work has been done with children from inner-city areas by the Outward Bound mountain and sailing schools. Yet access to the British countryside is still to a large degree the privilege of the white middle classes (Pendergast, 2004).

Outdoor adventurous activities have a long tradition in Britain. They have been influenced by Baden-Powell, who founded the Scout Movement, and the theories of Kurt Hahn, the originator of Outward Bound. Central to the thinking of Baden-Powell and Hahn was the idea that character is developed by experiencing and overcoming challenge. Mortlock (1984) has argued strongly in favour of allowing young people to have access to adventure for very similar reasons. Loynes (1996) has criticized the recent phenomenon of commercial corporations 'packaging' and marketing ready-made adventure opportunities, what he calls the 'McDonaldization' of adventure, on the grounds that it tends to diminish the agency of participants. There is much research (McKenzie, 2000; Rickinson et al., 2004) that suggests properly planned and managed outdoor adventurous activities can encourage a growth in self-confidence and self-esteem and other facets of self-concept. Mindful of these findings, many outdoor programmes have been developed for young people with 'difficulties': young offenders, 'disaffected' youth and their families. This type of remedial, or re-engagement, programme has arguably been simplified and trivialized by the *Brat Camps* TV series (www.channel4.com/life/microsites/B/bratcamp/). Yet claims of the efficacy of such programmes are widespread in outdoor literature (Rickinson et al., 2004). Academic underachievers have also been the target of outdoor programmes (Dismore and Bailey, 2005). Outdoor programmes have been set up for young women with eating disorders, with research findings suggesting these enabled them to cope better with their problems (Richards, 2001). One problem presented by these programmes has been that a different kind of exclusivity has developed, with outdoor learning opportunities seen as reserved only for learners with difficulties.

Other studies have pointed towards less tangible, but equally important and interesting benefits. For example, I have written about the role of outdoor experiences in promoting spiritual development (Rea, 2003), a theme also developed by Hitzhusen (2004); whilst Jacobs and colleagues (2004) have expanded research into outdoor learning by investigating outdoor programmes in relation to emotional intelligence (Goleman, 1996). Sue Waite and I have developed an argument for using the outdoors simply because it is enjoyable for both teacher and pupil (Rea and Waite, 2007). One thing that characterizes these studies is that they expand and broaden interpretations of inclusion and participation, arguing that outdoor learning is an entitlement for all and identifying obstacles to inclusion and participation.

Participation in informal learning outdoors: benefits and learner outcomes

Many claims have been made about the benefits of outdoor learning, and especially participation in adventurous activities. The value of outdoor learning opportunities is represented in a broad literature, useful summaries of which have been provided by McKenzie (2000) and Rickinson and colleagues (2004).

What is of great interest to mainstream educators and to students is that some studies suggest engagement with outdoor learning opportunities may have a positive effect on academic achievement. This is more than the adaptation of experiential pedagogies to classrooms, but rather taking or sending children away onto outdoor programmes. For example, Nundy (1999) shows that primary school children learn about physical geography better in the field than in the classroom; Christie (2004) reports academic gains in Scottish teenagers who took part in a programme aimed at those at risk of underachieving; and Dismore and Bailey (2005) point to the raised achievement of Key Stage 2 pupils who took part in targeted outdoor activities. Perhaps because of these claims, the government's manifesto for outdoor learning, produced as a well-meant reaction to the pervasive trend of passive, sedentary learning that does not suit all children, presents an argument for outdoor learning as an entitlement for all and states that 'learning outside the classroom is about raising achievement through an organised, powerful approach to learning in which direct experience is of prime importance' (DfES Teachernet, 2006).

Thus outdoor learning is now prescribed as an entitlement for all, an ideal few argue with. But it is also now defined in terms of the school improvement agenda, measuring achievement using the existing formal methods used in schools (Dismore and Bailey, 2005) in order to blend with the government's agenda. One danger of this is that informal, enjoyable learning that is fun may become formalized and prescriptive. In practice, despite government rhetoric about inclusion, many children are in danger of being excluded if this policy leads to a concentration of outdoor opportunities only for those who are deemed by schools to be underachieving. This is an interesting example of how government policy and agenda are quick to colonize the language of others: in this case that of inclusion. Other policies in education are in conflict with inclusion. This is exemplified in Chapter 1 where Gibson problematizes the juxtaposition of a neo-liberal standards policy with a humanitarian inclusion policy.

Current debates about challenge and risk in the outdoors and how this might affect participation

In the early spring of 2007 a teenage girl drowned in a Dartmoor river, swollen by extraordinarily heavy rain. She was training for the annual Ten Tors Challenge organized by the army. Ten Tors has taken place since 1961 and each year some 2,400 young people take part, spending a weekend walking 35, 45 or 55 miles over the moor, with full camping kit. It surely is a challenge. This was the first serious accident.

There will always be risks associated with taking children outdoors. There is a risk of physical harm ranging from very small injuries, such as a grazed arm or knee, to death. However, the probability of serious injury or death is very low indeed. It is certainly much lower than the risk of death or serious injury to a child incurred by crossing a road.

This small risk of harm should be set against two other factors:

- The risks incurred through a sedentary and over-protected lifestyle.
- The benefits of experiencing the outdoors.

When all of this is considered, even the most pessimistic outlook would find it difficult to argue against taking children outside in order to enrich their learning. Yet during the 1990s the number of children being taken outside school declined. The introduction by the government of the Manifesto for Outdoor Learning is a recent attempt to redress this situation.

Complacency should be avoided. Before any outdoor trip or activity is undertaken, a careful risk assessment should be carried out by somebody trained to do so. This should take into account any disabilities, learning difficulties and behavioural issues of the group.

A pedagogy for outdoor learning?

Kolb's (1984) theory has become a widely adopted pedagogic method. It underpins a number of practical models for use in the outdoors (Beard and Wilson, 2002). Amongst outdoor practitioners, 'processing' (Bacon, 1987) and 'reviewing' (Greenaway, 2002) are techniques now embedded in practice. Such approaches focus on experience plus discussion about the experience. They emphasize feedback, discussion and group processing practices. Many manuals for outdoor practitioners urge the promotion of reflective techniques. Ricketts and Willis (2001) have argued that practitioners ought to be extracting meaningful learning from experience, whilst Pfeiffer and Jones (1983) suggest that the processing modes of the experiential learning cycle are even more important than the experiencing stage.

This widespread acceptance and implementation of the Kolb (1984) model as a pedagogical approach has led to a high degree of proactive intervention by teachers, leaders and instructors on many programmes and has had the effect of formalizing outdoor learning. Critiques of this orthodoxy (Rea, 2007) suggest that these proactive group processing activities may be unnecessary and that learners are able to engage in reflective thinking about their experiences without formal reviewing activities.

Case study 1: The Gables

The Gables is a pseudonym for an outdoor education centre in England that is owned and administered by an English Local Authority (LA). Children reside at The Gables for five days in groups of up to thirty-four, accompanied by four teachers. The centre is staffed by the head and four other outdoor instructors (two of whom are qualified teachers) and support staff. Staff at The Gables feel pressurized by the LA into following practices that have become entrenched in the practice of schools. Thus they have defined a number of intended learning outcomes that all children are introduced to at the beginning of their residential experience. These are:

- *Making the future* relates to The Gables' eco-centre (Eco-Schools, 2002) status and ethos.

⇨

- *Caring, sharing and being a social being* relates to aspects of social learning; for example, team work and relationship nurturing.
- *Adventure for life* is mainly about the acquisition of those skills and attitudes deemed to be necessary for a full and active participatory lifestyle.
- *Risky business* is about doing things safely, emphasizing risk assessment and risk management.

Each of these intentions may be laudable. But Hayes has outlined the drawbacks of an over-formalized school curriculum that squeezes children's learning into 'predetermined packets' of time to meet learning objectives (2007: 151). He sees outdoor learning as a possible antidote to this. There is much evidence of the power of learning outside the classroom and the positive effects it may have on children. As one head teacher who regularly takes children to centres like this one told me, 'You know, it's this they will remember. Not the end-of-key stage tests or the literacy hour. The children come back to visit us years after they have left the school, and it's their visit to the [residential outdoor education] centre that they want to talk about' (Rea and Waite, 2007: 56). What a shame, then, that one of the first things children do at The Gables is sit for an hour listening to a presentation about the intended learning outcomes.

Education in England has become synonymous with schooling (Campbell, 2005) and schooling with organization and formality. The current orthodoxy and 'best practice' in English schools is for the teacher to organize every aspect of a child's learning. But Shepherd (2007) suggests there is probably no universal and absolute best practice in education, and if learning is seen as a theoretical concept (Stables, 2005), then best practice orthodoxy becomes problematic. To organize learning requires first that learning be reified and treated as a material or concrete thing. Nationally agreed and overly prescriptive curricula and pedagogy, the trend towards outcome testing and the perceived influence of external inspections have all contributed to this reification. It has meant that child-centred learning, with children passionately investigating problems that really interest them, has become a rarity (Hayes, 2007).

What is of even greater concern is the current 'best practice' mantra in English schools of teachers sharing their intended learning outcomes, often articulated in the bewildering language of the National Curriculum, with children (Hayes, 2007). This practice arguably commits children to a passive role. Nobody would object to teachers engaging in discussions with their pupils about what has been learnt, but this can be done in a more inclusive way, recognizing meaning, and therefore learning, filtered and constructed through multiple discourses in which children need to be active contributors.

If we accept that learning is a theoretical concept and that constructing meaning from experience may be a more useful way of thinking about it (Stables, 2005), then we are forced to recognize the active part the learner has to play in that constructive process (Re'em, 2001; Strauss and Quinn, 1997). Thus the orthodoxy of teachers attempting to organize all aspects of children's learning needs to be challenged.

Case study 2: Countryside College

Countryside College is a specialist post-16 college that accommodates the needs of around ninety teenagers with learning difficulties. A large number of their students have been diagnosed with autism or Asperger's syndrome – many are funded by local authorities, some by parents. The ethos and practices of the college, discussed below in some detail, follow Steiner principles. Most of the students return to their families during vacations, but a small number board at the college full time.

The college is housed in an old mill that was renovated by the founder and the first cohorts of young people. It is situated in large grounds that are used for farming, fishing and crafts. Making things from natural materials, using traditional tools and preserving traditional skills, movements[1] and names, and doing much of this in the outdoors, are central to the ethos of the Countryside College. This approach is based upon anthroposophic ideas. Anthroposophy is an approach to the understanding of the person and the spirit in a holistic way that brings together body, soul and mind. It was theorized by Rudolf Steiner (1995). Early in the twentieth century, when care for the physically challenged and those with learning difficulties was largely ignored in many countries, anthroposophical homes and communities were founded; for example, the Camphill Movement founded in Scotland. This has spread widely, and there are now well over a hundred Camphill communities and other anthroposophical homes for both children and adults in more than twenty-two countries around the world. Much of the ethos and practice of Countryside College are related to the ideas of such communities.

Anthroposophy is the philosophy that links:

- Steiner-Waldorf schools where an anthroposophical view and understanding of the human being is put into educational practice
- biodynamic, organic agriculture
- anthroposophical medicine
- Eurythmy, a Steiner art form which seeks to renew the spiritual foundations of dance, transforming speech and music into visible movement.

Many facets of the ethos and practice at Countryside College reflect and exemplify this philosophical approach. In addition the College believes that the students learn and develop through engaging with the environment in a meaningful way and by working with the variety of challenges that the natural environment and natural

⇨

materials present. Students practice organic agriculture and market gardening. They grow much of the organic produce for their own table and the onsite café that is open the public. Animals are bred, reared and killed, and then their hides are processed by students into leather products. A fish farm is located on campus. Trout are hatched, reared, caught, killed, smoked and eaten.

Green wood turning skills are practised. The wood is coppiced from sustainable woodland, planted and managed by the students. Iron is smelted in outdoor, traditional furnaces where students use hand bellows and tools to make simple products. On a recent visit there, I was shown a small knife, the pride of a teenage boy who had made the blade from metal he had smelted and fashioned and the hilt he had turned on a foot-operated lathe. Clay is collected from a bank. It is processed by hand, crafted using traditional throwing methods and then glazed and fired in kilns made by the students.

During their attendance at the college, usually three years, students will engage in all these outdoor activities. Other aspects of their holistic education, such as Eurythmy[1] and personal tutoring, are also addressed. In their final year, much of the emphasis is placed upon answering questions of progression: Where will the young person go once they leave the college? How will they support themselves in the outside world?

The work of Countryside College offers effective alternative pedagogies that widen participation and promote inclusion. Holistic, learner-centred, outdoor-based education is shown to be effective by the engagement and enjoyment of the learners, and by the degree to which students are able to participate in worthwhile occupations upon leaving the college.

Reflective exercises

1. Read Chapter 2 of Kaye Richards' (2001) book on adventure therapy and eating disorders. Reflect on the participation and inclusion issues embedded within the chapter (and book). You may like to think about Richards' feminization of both the body and eating disorders, and the effects of adventure therapy on inclusion in an outdoor sector with limited capacity.

2. Geoff Cooper's (1998) book contains many suggested activities for use with young people in the outdoors. Look at some of these activities (you may find others published elsewhere) and consider them in terms of inclusion issues. To what extent are they inclusive? If you find they are not, how might they be further adapted to encourage participation and inclusion?

3. Examine your own values in the context of outdoor learning, entitlement, participation and inclusion.

Author's note

I am passionate about the outdoors. I enjoy hills, moorland and mountains, and the sea. I began thinking about this chapter whilst taking part in the Tall Ships Race in August 2007, and drafted much of it whilst sailing across the North Sea. I love the outdoors and have strong beliefs about the positive contribution the outdoors can make to learning.

This began when I was 12 years old and a pupil at a boys' secondary modern school in Salford and went away for a week on an outdoor activities 'holiday' with the school. Later, when doing my CSEs, I learnt most of my physical geography outdoors in north Wales, then did an Outward Bound Course in the Lake District. Each time I was terribly homesick, often cold and wet and swore to myself that I would not do this again. But I kept coming back.

When I became a school teacher, I began to take young people out of school to participate in outdoor learning whenever I was able. I was convinced that opportunities to participate in outdoor experiences, and learn from these experiences, can and should be available to everyone, regardless of age, race, sex, mental or physical ability, class or socio-economic position. I still hold this conviction and the examples that I have chosen to use in this chapter reflect this.

I began researching my PhD, an ethnographic study of a residential outdoor education centre in 2004 (Rea, in progress). I now recognize things that concern me as outlined in this chapter and continue to see things that inspire me. On the whole, I remain optimistic about the future of informal learning outdoors and the possibilities for inclusion and participation that it holds.

Further reading

Cooper, G. (1998), *Outdoors with Young People*. Lyme Regis: Russell House Publishing.
Richards, K. (2001), *Adventure Therapy and Eating Disorders: A Feminist Approach to Research and Practice*. Ambleside: Brathy.

Note

1. By this I mean physical movements, especially big, slow, deliberate and rhythmic movements such as those involved in using a scythe or working a hand bellows. These are thought to have beneficial properties, especially useful in the management of some of the syndromes encountered by students at this college.

References

Bacon, S.B. (1987), *The Conscious Use of Metaphor in Outward Bound*. Denver, CO: Outward Bound School.
Baden-Powell, R.S.S. (1930), *Rovering to Success*. London: Herbert Jenkins Ltd.

Beard, C. and Wilson, J.P. (2002), *The Power of Experiential Learning, A Handbook for Trainers and Educators*. London: Kogan Page.

Campbell, R. (2005), 'Primary education or primary schooling?', *Education 3–13*, 33(1), 3–6.

Christie, E. (2004), 'Raising achievement through outdoor experiential learning? A case study of Scottish secondary school students'. Unpublished PhD, Edinburgh University.

Desforges, C. (1995), 'Learning out of school', in C. Desforges (ed.), *An Introduction to Teaching*. Oxford: Blackwell.

DfES Teachernet (2006), *Learning Outside the Classroom. Manifesto Summary*. London: DCSF. www.teachernet.gov.uk/teachingandlearning/resourcematerials/outsideclassroom/summary/ (accessed 30 July 2008).

Dismore, H. and Bailey, R. (2005), '"If only": outdoor and adventurous activities and generalised academic development', *Journal of Adventure Education and Outdoor Learning*, 5(1), 9–20.

Eco-Schools (2002), Home page. www.eco-schools.org.uk/ (accessed 17 January 2008).

Goleman, D. (1996), *Emotional Intelligence: Why it can Matter More than IQ*. London: Bloomsbury.

Greenaway, R. (2002), 'The active reviewing guide'. http://reviewing.co.uk/ (accessed 31 July 2006).

Hattie, J., Marsh, H., Neill, J. and Richards, G. (1997), 'Adventure education and outward bound: out-of-class experiences that make a lasting difference', *Review of Educational Research*, 67(1), 43–87.

Hayes, D. (2007), 'What Einstein can teach us about education', *Education 3–13*, 35(2), 143–154.

Hitzhusen, G. (2004), 'Understanding the role of spirituality and theology in outdoor environmental education: a mixed-method characterisation of 12 Christian and Jewish outdoor programs', *Research in Outdoor Education*, 7, 39–56.

Jacobs, J.A., McAvoy, L.H. and Bobilya, A.J. (2004), 'The relationship between summer camp employment and emotional intelligence', *Research in Outdoor Education*, 7, 73–89.

Kelly, P. (2007), 'The joy of enhancing children's learning', in D. Hayes (ed.), *Joyful Teaching and Learning in the Primary School*. Exeter: Learning Matters.

Kolb, D. (1984), *Experiential Learning: Turning Experience into Learning*. New Jersey: Prentice Hall.

Loynes, C. (1996), 'Adventure in a bun', *Journal of Adventure Education and Outdoor Leadership*, 13(2), 52–57.

McKenzie, M.D. (2000), 'How are adventure education program outcomes achieved? A review of the literature', *Australian Journal of Outdoor Education*, 5(1), 19–28.

Mortlock, C. (1984), *The Adventure Alternative*, Milnthorpe: Cicerone.

Nundy, S. (1999), 'The fieldwork effect: the role and impact of fieldwork in the Uer Primary School', *International Research in Geographical and Environmental Education*, 8(2), 190–198.

Pendergast, S. (2004), 'Social inclusion involving people from ethnic minorities in the Peak District National Park, England'. Paper presented at the Open Space, Edinburgh, UK.

Pfeiffer, J.W. and Jones, J.E. (1983), *The Annual Handbook for Group Facilitators*. John Wiley & Sons.

Re'em, M. (2001), 'Young minds in motion: interactive pedagogy in non-formal settings', *Teaching and Teacher Education,* 17, 291–305.

Rea, T. (2003), 'Why the outdoors may be an effective repository for spiritual development', *Horizons,* 23 (Summer), 12–14.

Rea, T. (2007), '"It's not as if we've been teaching them . . ." reflective thinking in the outdoor classroom', *Journal of Adventure Education and Outdoor Learning,* 6(2), 107–120.

Rea, T. (in progress), 'Understanding children's experiences at a residential outdoor education centre: from scientific "tales" to co-constructing fictionalised narratives'. Unpublished PhD, University of Plymouth, Exmouth.

Rea, T. and Waite, S. (2007), 'Enjoying teaching and learning outside the classroom', in D. Hayes (ed.), *Joyful Teaching and Learning in the Primary School*. Exeter: Learning Matters.

Richards, K. (2001), *Adventure Therapy and Eating Disorders: A Feminist Approach to Research and Practice*. Ambleside: Brathay.

Ricketts, M. and Willis, J. (2001), *Experience AI: A Practitioners Guide to Integrating Appreciative Inquiry with Experiential Learning*. Chagrin Falls, OH: Taos Institute.

Rickinson, M., Dillon, J., Teamey, K., Morris, M., Choi, M.Y., Sanders, D. et al. (2004), *A Review of Research on Outdoor Learning*. Shrewsbury: NFER/Field Studies Council.

Shepherd, I. (2007), 'Teaching and learning: do we really know what we are doing?' Paper presented at the University of Plymouth, VCs teaching and learning conference. http://intranet. plymouth.ac.uk/ (accessed 28 June 2007).

Stables, A. (2005), *Semiotic Engagement: A New Theory of Education*. Lewiston, NY: Mellen Press.

Steiner, R. (1995), *Anthroposophy in Everyday Life*. Hudson, NY: Anthroposophic Press.

Strauss, C. and Quinn, N. (1997), *A Cognitive Theory of Cultural Meaning*. Cambridge: Cambridge University Press.

'E's of Access: e-Learning and Widening Participation in Education

Steve Wheeler

9

Chapter Outline

The Information Age and the knowledge society	135
Digital divides	136
The 'e' is for everything	136
The nature of e-learning	138
Where does the learner fit into the 'e'quation?	139
E is for extended learning	140
E is for enhanced learning	141
E is for everywhere learning	142
E is for exclusion	143
Conclusion	144
Author's note	144

Support for university students has been radically transformed because of the proliferation of digital technologies. The advent of the Internet, mobile technologies and ubiquitous computing affords possibilities previously inconceivable. In this chapter we examine the technological trends and identify several key areas in which students are engaging with learning through what has been termed 'e-learning'. This chapter examines definitions of e-learning, and evaluates its contribution to widening participation and the provision of greater access to learning opportunities.

The Information Age and the knowledge society

The proliferation of digital technologies towards the end of the last century persuaded Castells (1996) to call this era the 'Information Age'. In doing so he evinced the notion that information conveyed within networks would assume more importance for society than the transportation of materials and goods. Castells (2000) believes that the information society we now occupy is the product of the historical convergence not only of technologies, but also of social movements and economic systems. Such convergence prompted a meeting in Lisbon of the European Council in March 2000. There they set a strategic goal for the first decade of the new millennium, in which Europe would aim to become the most competitive and dynamic knowledge economy in the world. This would be achieved through sustainable economic growth and prosperity brought about through a transformation of the educational system, and information technology would play a key role in the establishment of a knowledge society (Punie, 2007).

Whether or not this goal has been achieved, many would agree that information and communication technologies (ICTs) have made a profound impact upon society. Digital telecommunications can connect people to each other, to interactive experiences and to digital learning resources wherever they are, whenever they want. Digital media are able to convey entertainment and news across the globe, and all of this functionality has converged into a single platform – the Internet.

Since the mid-1990s, the Internet has become increasingly pervasive, gaining a strong purchase over all aspects of life, including leisure, business, health and, significantly, education. Such is our societal dependence that it is now hard to imagine a world in which there is no 'network of networks' or a society in which e-mail and instant messaging are absent. Such applications have become an integral part of the fabric of educational institutions worldwide and universities are exploiting their power to provide rich social contact for distributed students. There are also many ways in which technology can support, or in some cases actually enable learning, providing access which would previously have been difficult or impossible. For example, students who have severe visual impairment can be equipped with text-to-voice software which 'speaks' out the words on the screen. Such assistive technologies have revolutionized education by opening up new opportunities that previously would have been impossible or problematic.

Digital divides

There are of course many divisions in society that derive directly or indirectly from the rapid proliferation of digital technologies. Referred to widely as 'the digital divide', this exclusion can be identified at several levels. There are the 'haves and have nots', the latter being those who are excluded from full participation in the knowledge society because of socio-economic constraints. Another level is the 'can and cannot' level. Many students either do not have the pre-requisite skills to use technology effectively, or they cannot access specific training opportunities. Finally, there is a psychological dimension, which we can refer to as the 'wills and will nots'. The 'will nots' part of the population may suffer from technophobia, which is a spectrum of responses to technology from mild frustration to abject rejection (Brosnan, 1999). All the digital divides mentioned have the potential to exclude potential users from full participation in the knowledge society, resulting in long-term detrimental problems for learning. The critical question of what constitutes barriers and divides in education is exemplified further by Haynes in Chapter 5.

The need to provide better access to higher education has never been greater and is not simply a legislative requirement as seen in the Disability Discrimination Act (DDA) and the Special Educational Needs and Disability Act (SENDA). It is also a need based upon economically sustainable futures and the continued wellbeing of the knowledge society. It is generally acknowledged by many commentators and successive governments that a highly educated population is more successful on the economic world stage and that e-learning has a prominent role to play in this:

> Technology has an important role to play in the development and sustainability of the knowledge society, and is a key feature of lifelong learning. The term 'e-learning' has been introduced to describe 'any learning experience that utilises . . . technologies to some extent'.
>
> (Weller, 2007: 5)

The 'e' is for everything

In 2000 Richard Katz and Diana Oblinger published an edited volume entitled *The 'E' is for Everything*. Reminiscent of Castells conceptualization, the book presented a manifesto for the future of education premised on a convergence of e-learning, e-commerce and e-business and firmly rooted within the information society. In essence, Katz and Oblinger were proposing a technologically enhanced transformation of existing educational practices. One of their core arguments was that the Internet would fundamentally change the face of education as we perceived it, ushering in a new landscape of pedagogical thinking, practice and culture. They predicted that whilst traditional learning modes would continue to be offered for years to come, new approaches to offering and consuming education would increase (Katz and Oblinger, 2000). For Katz and Oblinger, e-learning would become all pervasive, ubiquitous and indispensable. The 'e' would become the new 'killer application', encompassing and eclipsing all other forms of education.

Many teachers bridled at this prospect. Some feared that the long, illustrious history and cherished mores of traditional teaching would be eroded through some kind of 'McDonaldization' process – a needless trivialization and homogenization of the fundamental human right of education (Bryson, 2004). Others simply refused to accept that it would happen.

We are now observing an inexorable move by all UK higher and further education institutes towards e-learning initiatives which exploit a variety of digital media and technologies to enhance and extend educational provision. There is scarcely a further or higher education institute within the UK that does not have an e-learning strategy embedded somewhere within its mission statement. By 2003, 86 per cent of British higher education institutions were using a virtual learning environment or 'VLE' (Weller, 2007). In 2004 Becta reported that more than 70 per cent of UK further education colleges had a proprietary virtual learning environment. Observing technological trends, we may safely assume that in the intervening time since these reports, percentages have increased. For many, the driving force for VLE adoption is financial, and for too few, issues of quality and access have become the central concern. For others, e-learning is becoming an essential corporate strategy for survival as mega-universities begin to invade traditional catchment areas of the smaller institutions (Wheeler, 2004). In 2000 I presented a keynote address to the European Universities (EUCEN) conference in Bergen, Norway. My keynote was entitled 'The traditional university is dead: long live the distributed university' (Wheeler, 2000). I was deliberately contentious, which ensured that my speech was met equally by consternation and excitement. However, my main theme was serious – that many colleges and universities will simply not survive in the stringent climate of the new knowledge economy unless there is substantial investment in distributed approaches to learning which make effective use of e-learning methods.

Patently e-learning has its fierce critics as well as its devoted adherents. Technology-supported education has become a battlefield. At Stanford University, commenting on the mixed reception given to Internet search engines, Sergei Brin declared that some saw Google as God, others as Satan. The academic press is replete with articles extolling the virtues of e-learning, or highlighting many of its inherent pitfalls. The criticism extends to current laissez-faire student attitudes, including the Internet 'cut and paste' culture which leads to accusations of plagiarism, and over reliance on websites such as Wikipedia, which are openly editable by all, and therefore prone to inaccuracy and unsubstantiated opinion. This has led to the denouncement of open content websites, and claims that they trivialize knowledge and undermine the authority of acknowledged experts (Keen, 2007).

It would therefore be naïve or even dangerous to assume that technology provides all the answers, but its presence does enable us to ask some of the right questions. In spite of all the hyperbole, questionable motives and claims over the trivialization of education, technology-supported learning yields a range of potential benefits that demand to be evaluated. To undertake this task, we must grasp both the nature and the ethos of e-learning.

The nature of e-learning

So what exactly is the 'e' for? Most would agree that the 'e' in e-learning stands for 'electronic', and this was its earliest direction. E-learning presents education within the scope for an entire spectrum of new or modified pedagogical practice, challenges and agencies. Since the days of the first telephones, electronic technologies have been used to mediate communication between separated individuals and down the years a whole plethora of technologies, from radio, television, audio and videoconferencing, computer-mediated communication and streaming media have been tried and tested in the educational arena. The virtual learning environment (VLE) seems to be a nexus of all these and is for now, at least, the *de rigueur* incarnation of e-learning.

Academics have studied each technology in turn, trawling for evidence of benefits and limitations, in a perpetual quest for the 'perfect' educational technology. Ultimately, there is disagreement about whether technologies actually enhance and influence learning, or whether they are simply a transportation method to convey learning materials to students. There is an ongoing debate about the nature and affordances of technology. Clark (1994), for example, suggests that media and technology do not influence learning, but are in fact neutral and 'mere vehicles' to deliver learning materials. Kozma (1994), by contrast, argues that technologies cannot be neutral, because each possesses unique affordances that influence the experiences of the learner. Such affordances describe the expectations of the student about what the technology can do for them, derived from the manner in which the technology is presented. There is also debate about exactly how computers and technologies should be best used to enhance and extend the learning experience. Jonassen (1999, 2000) argues that computers have yet to be used effectively to extend the learning experience. He criticizes the computer assisted learning (CAL) model in which the computer 'teaches' the student. He holds the view that computers have better 'memories' than humans and humans can teach better than computers. His proposition is therefore to reverse the CAL model, so that humans 'teach the machine' to remember all they have learned, and in so doing, extend their own memory, thereby freeing up their cognitive resources. Ostensibly, this is now beginning to happen in the so-called 'social web', where user-generated content and the sharing of digital artefacts are contemporary practice for many younger Internet users (Kamel Boulos et al., 2006).

Some commentators view the rapid development of digital media and e-learning as essential to the continued defining of culture (de Kerckhove, 1997), whilst others see the use of computers as a natural part of the human evolutionary process (Clark, 2003). Most would agree, however, that although it may be contentious, e-learning in all of its various guises is here to stay, and does not show signs of going away. What is also clear is that researchers should continually investigate the many ways in which it can be used to improve educational practice, enhance learning and widen participation for lifelong learners.

Where does the learner fit into the 'e'quation?

Deciding that the 'e' in e-learning stands solely for 'electronic' does education something of disfavour. It confines learning within the boundaries of a technocentric, hybrid version of education. If the 'e' in e-learning merely represents technology, then where does the learner fit into the equation?

Does e-learning imply that learning is driven by technology with the consequence that the learner is merely a passive recipient of knowledge?

This argument can also be extended to the concept of 'knowledge media'. Is the media there simply to transmit 'knowledge' or should it be applied as David Jonassen and his colleagues (1999) have recommended, as a 'mindtool' to enable learners to extend their cognitive abilities. ICT has the potential to create environments conducive to the promotion of learning that is powerful and individualized. It also proffers unprecedented opportunities to connect students together so that collaborative and cooperative learning can be supported regardless of location. E-learning should be viewed as infinitely more than mere technology, or in the words of Richard Clark 'mere vehicles' to deliver learning (Clark, 1994). In this chapter, we shall continue by exploring some of the wider possibilities of e-learning and how it may be instrumental in widening participation for the next generation of lifelong learners.

E is for extended learning

The technologies and media employed in e-learning can be used to extend learners' experiences, providing opportunities to learn in ways that suit student lifestyles, preferences and contexts. This extension of possibilities also relates to a widening of participation in which many more have the opportunity to participate within the knowledge society, because the traditional barriers are being broken down.

Such barriers to full participation in lifelong learning include physical disability, socio-economic status, geographical location, age and domestic demands such as childcare and work commitments. The introduction of open learning approaches through a combination of face-to-face learning and distance education have transformed learning opportunities for many. I am referring here to 'blended learning', an increasingly popular approach for universities and colleges which combines face-to-face education with flexible alternatives that are usually located outside the traditional boundaries of the institution.

Students who are not able to attend their parent educational institution can study at a distance from home or in the workplace whilst still connecting to tutors, resources and fellow learners as required. Students who have domestic or employment commitments during the day can time-shift their studies to the evening or weekends, accessing asynchronous learning networks to maintain the impetus of their programme of study. Rich discourse and detailed feedback can be received from peers and tutors through e-mail or conferencing. E-learning affords remote students the chance to engage in communities of practice from wherever and whenever. Students are not precluded from attending college or university, but extended learning makes the time and place of study more convenient for the individual. There is often criticism of the efficacy of blended approaches. The premier objection is that tutor–student dialogue is constrained by reduced social cues and loss of immediacy when conversations are mediated through technology. Indeed, it does appear that student drop-out rates are higher when students study exclusively at a distance from the parent organization (Simpson, 2003). However, there is a large body of research extending over thirty years suggesting that there is no significant difference between the quality of the experiences of on-campus and remote students (Merisotas and Phipps, 1999).

E is for enhanced learning

Enhancing the student learning experience is a task permanently incumbent upon all teachers and lecturers. As professional practitioners we all strive for quality, and to this end we should reflect regularly and critically upon and through our practice. Evaluative strategies are generally designed to detect and eradicate weaknesses, and strengthen positive aspects of course design and provision. For many, because of its versatility, e-learning has the potential to enhance the learning experience beyond recognition. The use of online diaries or blogs, for example, can encourage deeper reflection on practice through self-disclosure (Qian and Scott, 2007), and a reportage that can be creatively richer than paper-based recordings (Pederson and Macafee, 2007).

The use of social software can facilitate peer support that is enhanced beyond the traditional experience of the classroom. Potential students often veer away from lifelong learning opportunities simply though a fear of failure. They are anxious about returning to an environment in which they may previously have failed as learners, or in which they had poor experiences of pedagogy. Poor self-concept and a lack of self-esteem are often reasons for self-exclusion. Some people feel it is too late to return to study and that the opportunity has passed them by. Many, however, encounter the Open University, an institution founded on distance education. The OU has been dubbed the 'University of the second chance' because it is never too late to learn, and many mature students have been able to rediscover the joy of learning through its open doors policy and flexibly delivered courses.

Widening participation is one positive outcome and an expedient one. Thanks to organizations such as the OU, students who had previously been excluded or disenfranchised from further and higher education are now able to access learning, enabling them to follow their choice of studies using adaptive, specially designed media and technology. Dyslexic students and those with visual impairment, for example, can access text-based systems that offer adjustable text size, font and colour. Voice-to-text and text-to-voice software are further useful applications to enhance student learning opportunities. E-learning can deliver outreach programmes to isolated rural communities, transforming lives and enhancing careers. The Welsh ALPs project, RATIO in southwest England, and the Highlands and Islands project in Scotland are classic examples of this kind of technology-based training provision (Wheeler, 2005). They provide technology-based solutions to the access issues experienced by isolated communities and, in effect, where work-based training is concerned, such projects level the playing field for small businesses located in remote rural areas.

E is for everywhere learning

The world is a large place, but we perceive it to be rapidly shrinking as telecommunication technologies are refined and made more easily accessible, international travel becomes cheaper and easier, and the process of globalization becomes ever more trenchant. Media was once hailed as the means to bring the world into the classroom. This ideal can now be challenged – surely multi-media now have the potential to take the classroom out into the world, and for many students this is becoming a reality, albeit a virtual one.

Students can visit museums on several continents, travel to the depths of the Mariana Trench, and then pay a visit to the dark side of the moon using virtual tour software, or 3-D multi-user virtual environments such as Second Life. Using digitally generated simulations, biology students can ride on the back of a blood corpuscle as it travels through the circulatory system, and physics students can explore the infinitesimally small centre of an atom. Through video-links, trainee surgeons can observe live surgical procedures anywhere in the world, viewing operations as if they were physically present and performing the surgery themselves courtesy of the surgeon's head-mounted camera. Alternative perspectives might be available from inside the patient via tiny fibre-optic cameras. Trainees can enjoy live dialogue with the surgeon as a particular procedure is explained, and all this can be experienced without them travelling more than a few feet from their own patients.

The same, of course, can apply to education studies and there are many areas of teacher education and training that would benefit from the application of appropriate digital technologies. Educators adopting technology-mediated experiential learning approaches must, of course, heed the potential cultural differences that exist in our increasingly connected and globalized society. Language and the conveyance of images and sounds all own the potential to be variously interpreted, or indeed misunderstood if they are used insensitively. If these potential barriers are successfully managed however, it appears that the only limitations that remain exist within the minds of teacher educators. With a modicum of creativity and a little time and effort, most experiences can be replicated for those who cannot attend the university or school in person.

E is for exclusion

I will reiterate my concerns here about the less positive aspects of e-learning. The digital divide in all its guises can and does exclude potential students from full participation in the knowledge society, but this is by no means its full negative impact. All technology can be used for good, but all can also be used nefariously. Rising cases of cyber-bullying have featured in recent press articles. Social networking sites, chat rooms and text messages to mobile telephones have all been used to ridicule, intimidate and threaten children in and outside of schools. These are direct malicious uses of ICTs and they serve to isolate students and, ultimately, force them to exclude themselves from full participation in learning. More indirectly, uses of mobile phone cameras to video physical assaults on vulnerable children in 'happy slapping' incidents have also been reported. Such cases are not, of course, limited to technology, and indeed many bullying incidents are independent of ICTs, but it should be acknowledged that digital technologies can make it easier for bullying to occur, not least because of their speed and easy access and their ability to mask identities.

Such incidents have led schools to ban the use of mobiles in schools and to block the use of certain social networking tools and websites from the classroom. Although expedient to protect the vulnerable and limit the potential for abuse, such decisions in themselves arguably exclude children from benefiting from the huge learning potential of digital technologies.

Conclusion

With the advent of new mobile technologies, advanced telecommunication networks, broadband and wireless connectivity, intelligent agents and a variety of handheld and wearable technologies, everywhere learning is set to radically transform the way we conceive, practise and consume education. We should take care, however, to ensure that the new technologies that are introduced into the classroom are used appropriately, and sensitively, taking students' needs, styles and individual differences into account. If used inappropriately, ICTs can have detrimental effects, leading to marginalization, isolation and exclusion. If used effectively, ICTs can transform the learning experience, engaging students more deeply and encouraging creativity. If teachers manage to achieve this, then perhaps we will witness the 'everything' of e-learning originally espoused by Katz and Oblinger.

Author's note

I have been privileged to be an eye-witness to the rapid evolution of new learning technologies over the past thirty years, and have watched as we have been ushered into the Information Age. Throughout my entire career I have taken on the role of change agent – it has been my job to introduce emerging digital technologies into the classroom and to train teachers to get the best out of them. It now appears that just about everything found within the classroom can be delivered or managed through digital technology. However, this has come with a price.

I was there when the first personal computers were introduced into schools, and heard some teachers express their fears about being 'replaced'. To assuage their fears I remember quoting the celebrated science fiction writer Arthur C. Clarke, who declared 'Any teacher who can be replaced by a computer . . . should be.' It hit home, and the teachers realized that computers were there to support them, not supplant them. I believe also that this was the first time I myself began clearly to appreciate that learning technologies (what we also refer to as information and communication technologies or ICTs) were merely tools to enable and facilitate learning. They are very sophisticated and powerful tools, but still tools nevertheless. I was also there when the World Wide Web was birthed, and watched as it quickly became the 'killer application' that would replace many other well-established learning resources. Now I am witnessing the deep and far-reaching impact of mobile and wireless technologies, social networking services and classroom-based technologies such as the interactive whiteboard. As I observe, I notice that professional practice, teacher roles and student experiences are all being transformed.

These changes are all-pervasive and, to many teachers, just as disconcerting as the time the first computers were introduced into the classroom. When I first entered the world of learning technologies I knew very little, and my learning curve was steep. I felt like an outsider looking in, and worked hard to 'learn my trade'. Thirty years on, the learning curve is still rising, and I find that I have to run hard in order to keep up with the pace of the change. I am expected to, because I am an ICT specialist, an insider. This leads to a number of problems, one of which is my need to continually update myself on 'what is new'. Because I am now 'inside' I often risk losing sight of the 'big picture' as I focus on new technologies. I constantly have to remind myself that ICTs are still only tools and that the 'learning' comes before 'technology' for a very good reason. They are tools that have inherent advantages and disadvantages, and they still have the power to exclude or include. They are tools that evoke a number of emotional responses from students and staff alike, some positive and some less so.

ICTs are tools for learning and for teaching, tools that enable better communication, quicker access to resources and, ultimately, tools that have the potential to include everyone in the wonderful experience of learning something new. Although I am now an insider, I know that there are many who feel themselves to be outsiders. Whatever the 'e' now stands for in e-learning, it certainly stands for 'eclectic' for there have never been so many methods of delivery available to the teacher as there are today. If there is a strap line for my chapter, it is this: as well as its power to widen participation, e-learning has the potential to marginalize some students and teachers, and it is the wise practitioner who realizes this and manages to use technology appropriately.

References

Becta, (2004), 'A review of the research literature on the use of managed learning environments in education'. www.partners.becta.org.uk/page_documents/research/VLE_report. pdf (accessed 13 February 2007).

Brosnan, M.J. (1999), *Technophobia*. London: Routledge.

Bryson, C. (2004), 'What about the workers? The expansion of higher education and the transformation of academic work', *Industrial Relations Journal*, 35(1), 38–57.

Castells, M. (1996), *The Information Age: Economy, Society and Culture: Volume 1: The Rise of the Networked Society*. Oxford: Blackwell.

Castells, M. (2000), *The Information Age: Economy, Society and Culture: Volume 3: End of Millennium*. 2nd edn. Oxford: Blackwell.

Clark, A.J. (2003), *Natural-Born Cyborgs: Minds, Technologies and the Future of Human Intelligence*. New York: Oxford University Press.

Clark, R.E. (1994), 'Media will never influence learning', *Education Technology Research and Development*, 42(2), 21–29.

de Kerckhove, D. (1997), *The Skin of Culture: Investigating the New Electronic Reality*. London: Kogan Page.

Jonassen, D.H. (2000), *Computers as Mind Tools for Schools*. Upper Saddle River, NJ: Prentice Hall.

Jonassen, D.H., Wilson, B. and Peck, K. (1999), *Learning with Technology*. Upper Saddle River, NJ: Prentice Hall.

Kamel Boulos, M.N., Maramba, I. and Wheeler, S. (2006), 'Wikis, blogs and podcasts: a new generation of web-based tools for virtual collaborative clinical practice and education', *BMC*

Medical Education, 6(41). Online at: www.biomedcentral.com/1472-6920/6/41 (accessed 30 November 2006).

Katz, R. and Oblinger, D. (eds), (2000), *The 'E' is for Everything: E-commerce, E-Business, and E-Learning in the Future of Higher Education.* Educause Leadership Strategies: Volume 2. San Francisco: Jossey Bass.

Keen, A. (2007), *The Cult of the Amateur: How Today's Internet is Killing Our Culture and Assaulting Our Economy.* London: Nicholas Brealey.

Kozma, R.B. (1994), 'Will media influence learning? Reframing the debate', *Education Technology Research and Development*, 42(1), 7–19.

Merisotas, J.P. and Phipps, R.A. (1999), 'What's the difference? Outcomes of distance v. traditional classroom-based learning', *Change*, 31(3), 13–17.

Pederson, S. and Macafee, C. (2007), 'Gender differences in British blogging', *Journal of Computer-Mediated Communication*, 12, 1472–1492.

Punie, Y. (2007), 'Learning spaces: an ICT-enabled model of future learning in the knowledge-based society', *European Journal of Education*, 42(2), 185–199.

Qian, H. and Scott, C.R. (2007), 'Anonymity and self-disclosure on weblogs', *Journal of Computer-Mediated Communication*, 12, 1428–1451.

Simpson, O. (2003), *Student Retention in Online, Open and Distance Learning.* London: RoutledgeFalmer.

Weller, M. (2007), *Virtual Learning Environments: Using, Choosing and Developing your VLE.* London: Routledge.

Wheeler, S. (2000), 'The traditional university is dead: Long live the distributed university'. Keynote speech to the EUCEN Conference, University of Bergen, Norway. May. Online at: www2.plymouth.ac.uk/distancelearning/steve.html (accesses 18 September 2007).

Wheeler, S. (2004), 'Five smooth stones: fighting for the survival of higher education'. *Distance Learning*, 1(3), 11–17.

Wheeler, S. (2005), 'British distance education: a proud tradition', in Y. Visser, L. Visser and M. Simonson (eds), *Trends and Issues in Distance Education: An International Perspective.* Greenwich, CT: Information Age Publisher.

Widening Participation in Adult Education

Roger Cutting

Chapter Outline

The Parents as Educators Programme   153
Getting going   153
The course design   154
Recruitment   155
Unlocking the door   157
The 'R' word – retention issues   159
The end   160
Evaluating a programme   160
Conclusions   161
Author's note   164

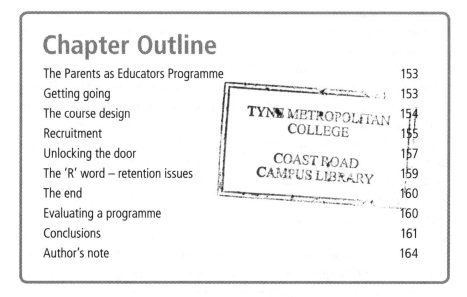

This chapter deals with some of the issues surrounding widening participation for socially excluded adult students in education. This is a complex topic and what follows is not a definitive exploration, rather an overview of the changing nature of adult education followed by a case example of a project. This case highlights some of the current challenges and problems surrounding implementation.

If you are an undergraduate student in a UK university, the chances are that you too are defined as an 'adult learner'. Consequently, this presents a good opportunity for you to reflect on your own experiences of inclusion in this area. Before reading further consider the specific example of yourself. On occasion, throughout this chapter, you will be addressed directly as a reader and invited to think of your own aims and motivations for learning as an adult. What were the motivations that brought you to further study? Perhaps you have one eye on the employment market and hope to get a good job when you graduate, or perhaps you were just drawn to further learning. These two motivations are not the only ones, nor are they mutually exclusive, but they do introduce two important, and increasingly disparate, areas of adult education. One is vocational and/or skills-based learning, based around the further education (FE) sector, and the other a broader educational, possibly even non-certificated, area of provision, tending to be based around community or adult education centres. At times of downturn of the seemingly cyclical priority of funding in adult education, it is really no surprise that the latter provision experiences the greatest pressure and yet historically this is where the origins of adult education lie (Field, 2006).

R.H. Tawney (1880–1962), described by Elsey (1987) as the patron saint of adult education, argued that social justice was inextricably linked to widening participation in education (Tawney, 1964). He saw the great social movements of the nineteenth century as not only social but also great educational movements (Taylor, 2007). Interestingly, in his writings on education, not only does he point out the importance of adult education as a means of achieving social justice, but he also talks of the commitment of those delivering such classes, suggesting that such involvement is driven by more than any personal gain, and that these teachers 'become partners in a universe of interests' (Tawney, 1950). He was also on the executive of the Workers Educational Association (WEA) for forty-two years and often taught adult groups. The students in his session were described by Kelly: 'They came in search of knowledge, not certificates, and their interest was principally in political and social subjects . . . The enthusiasm and determination of the students was tremendous' (1970: 254).

A review of R.H. Tawney's work provides an interesting philosophical base for work on widening participation. Intriguing are two observations which resonate with the contemporary: the commitment of teachers, 'friends being taught by friends' as he described it, and the enthusiasm of students. Arguably, nothing much has changed. As a practitioner, it is undoubtedly the case that the adult education and Further Education sectors are populated by people who have dedicated their careers to widening participation. Indeed, one could reasonably argue that the raison d'etre of adult education is to provide access to those outside the 'traditional' provision. It is curious to note that the innovative and creative approaches to teaching and learning associated with this frequently forgotten sector have been developed and delivered throughout the lifetimes of successive governments and long before 'inclusion' became stated policy.

The Adult group dynamic is a peculiar and precious one. Adult students frequently require help and support in building confidence but equally can be overly lively. In the animated film *Shrek*, Princess Fiona expresses her amazement at Donkey's ability to talk. 'Oh aye,' replies Shrek, 'the trick is getting him to shut up'. Most adult educators empathize with that sentiment sooner or later.

Despite the contemporary resonance of Tawney's comments on the nature of teachers and adult learners, the greatest modern difference lies with the underlying aims of adult education. Ideas on it being a tool for emancipation and social justice seem to have been replaced by an economic imperative. This may be best illustrated by briefly thinking back to your own motivations for studying: are they economic, in the sense that you wish to gain a good job, or are you learning for other reasons beyond those related to your employment prospects? Quite reasonably, you may well plump for a mixture of the two, but which do you see as predominant? If you see employment as one of your main reasons for studying, then you are very much in line with the thinking behind many government reports over the last decade. These have promoted a view of 'inclusion' that implies social inclusion is achieved through economic participation. People are empowered to take an active part in the economy. The following passage epitomize Tawney's thoughts on education:

> the process by which we transcend the barriers of our isolated personalities, and become partners in a universe of interests which we share with our fellow men, living and dead alike. No one can be fully at home in the world unless, through some acquaintance with literature and art, the history of society and the revelations of science, he has seen enough of the triumphs and tragedies of mankind to realize the heights to which human nature can rise and the depths to which it can sink.
>
> (1950: 6)

For him and his contemporaries, education was about transcendence: a means of escaping from the confines of class and social bigotry. Indeed, adult education in particular was a primary mechanism for collective liberation, what we are more likely today to call 'social inclusion'. We should carefully consider the current onus on economic empowerment through more vocational education. Is it the equal, or indeed is it more efficacious, in achieving wider participation in society than the social emancipation perspective of adult education prevalent in the first half of the twentieth century?

This shift has been a fairly recent event. Indeed, the incoming Labour government of 1997 had a commitment to widening participation in education, particularly at a community level. In 1998 the government Green Paper *The Learning Age* (DfEE, 1998) was published, setting out the then new government's priorities for adult education. To get an impression of the content of this document it is worth reading the Foreword (written by the then Secretary of State for Education and Employment, David Blunkett) and the introduction for Section 2 (the document is available online and can be found at www.lifelonglearning.co.uk/greenpaper/ch0002.htm). The Foreword talks of 'The fostering of an enquiring mind and the love of learning' being essential prerequisites for a successful future. In the introduction to Section 2 it argues that 'the development of a culture of learning will help to build a united society' and that learning provides benefits on a number of different levels. At the individual level, learning 'offers excitement and the opportunity for discovery. It stimulates enquiring minds and nourishes our souls.' At a community level, learning 'contributes to social cohesion and fosters a sense of belonging, responsibility and identity'. At a national level it is 'essential to a strong economy and an inclusive society' and it talks of the importance of bridging 'the learning divide', that is, the gap between those who have benefited from learning and those who have not.

It was a powerful, even inspirational statement, widely welcomed by those employed in the further and adult education sectors. What resulted from this Green Paper will be discussed shortly, but before that, it is important to note that the ideas put forward in *The Learning Age* were influenced by the conclusions of two earlier highly influential government reports, *Inclusive Learning* and *Learning Works*. Here, referred to simply as they became known, namely the Tomlinson Report (FEFC, 1996) and the Kennedy Report (Kennedy, 1997).

The Tomlinson Report dealt with issues concerning those students with disabilities and/or difficulties associated with learning. It recognized that creating separate provision and providing 'special' education for such students was failing in a number of ways and those educational institutions, especially in the FE sector, needed to respond by providing routes, not into special classes, but into mainstream provision. This would necessarily require a refocusing of teaching and learning which would be based on the requirements of the individual, so-called 'inclusive learning'. Within the FE sector inclusive learning was not only concerned with physical access to facilities and courses, a very marked outcome in following years as considerable funding was provided to carry out building work required to adapt colleges, but also the redesigning of provision in terms of organization, assessment and, most importantly, teaching and learning. It needed to provide at an individual level for the learning styles and requirements of all students, traditional and non-traditional. In short, it was not just about widening door frames; it was about widening learning, challenging the status quo and traditional perceptions of learners with disabilities.

This is a very important point, as in other educational contexts, such as those described by Gibson in Chapter 1 of this book, inclusion will often be related to social inclusion, promoting community involvement and local engagement (Florian, 1998; Rosenthal, 2001; Gibson and Blandford, 2005). Conversely, the emphasis in the FE sector was to relate inclusive learning styles within the institutions rather than to any kind of wider social agenda.

The Kennedy Report (Kennedy, 1997) argued that both inclusive learning and wider, social inclusion are inseparable. It is perhaps easier to see how this could be more the case in the mainstream school sector, with a broader social curriculum and 'captive' client group, schools are often seen as communities in their own right and community involvement is formally encouraged. In the adult education and FE sectors, the delineation seems far more apparent and even this much-heralded report places an emphasis on the importance of learning skills as the driver for integration. As the Kennedy Report argues:

> the achievement of economic goals and social cohesion are intertwined. A healthy society is a necessary condition for a thriving economy: where parents encourage and support their children's education; where people in employment can adapt to change; where enterprise can flourish and where those seeking employment can acquire the skills they need for economic activity.
>
> (Kennedy, 1997: 16)

'The Learning Age' begins with a quote from Tony Blair stating 'Education is the best economic policy we have.' This rather succinctly summarizes the view that social exclusion is most effectively fought through the economic emancipation of people achieved through the development of skills and training, but consider the language and high ideals of 'The Learning Age'. Is the type of learning which develops 'enquiring minds' and provides 'nourishment for our souls' really provided by an adult education sector supplying vocational skills and training as part of an economic imperative required for a successful economy?

The late 1990s and early 2000s witnessed a marked and impressive increase in adult participation in UK universities in part arising from significant growth in Access programmes and more recently foundation degrees (HEFCE, 2008). Yet since 2005, there has been marked reduction of funding for Access programmes in the FE sector and a much greater emphasis on Level 2 and vocational training (Summers, 2007). A problem relating to the provision of skills is that the skills needs of local communities are complex and geographically variable. As a result, national funding organizations have to be flexible and responsive to these local conditions. The Learning and Skills Act (2000) addressed this issue changing the funding of the FE sector by replacing the Further Education Funding Council (FEFC) and the Training and Enterprise Councils (TECs) with one funding body: the Learning and Skills Council (LSC). A national organization now based (since 2004) on nine English regions (within which there are forty-seven local offices) with, in 2006–7 a budget of £10.4 billion (Learning and Skills Council, 2007). The secretaries of state for the Department for Children, Schools and Families (DCSF) and for the Department for Innovation, Universities and Skills jointly produce an annual 'Grant Letter' setting out both the annual budget and the government's skills priorities. The LSCs then effectively buy courses from local providers to meet these aims through funding programmes such as Local Initiative Fund (LIF) Projects.

So we have a system dedicated to greater inclusion and participation, but one which is very much based on skills, particularly vocational ones. The development of skills-based provision for those who are socially and economically excluded should lead to a greater sense of inclusion and community.

The provision of vocational education and training is unquestionably valuable. Yet, there is the danger of losing sight of the equal value of non-vocational adult education. The push for skills and training resulting in present initiatives, such as Skills Plus and Train to Gain, has come to dominate many aspects of adult provision, particularly as funding in recent years has moved away from adult education and has resulted in a drastic reduction of courses being offered (Tucket, 2008).

Think about the following question. What are the values of non-vocational adult education courses? The following case example will hopefully help you formulate some views as its aims were not vocational. There were learning outcomes certainly, which concerned 'understanding' and 'application', but there were also deeper, less easily evaluated, emergent outcomes. These were based around notions such as building confidence, overcoming the stigma associated with learning and promoting social networks. It is best summed up by the programme coordinator discussing her involvement in the 'Parents as Educators' programme: 'we just wanted a course that would let young parents learn how to be with their children' (Desira, 2003: 15). To reach these groups and promote such courses, particularly as they are not 'vocational', requires specific strategies. Such strategies and their relative effectiveness are discussed here through an illustrative case example. Throughout, a checklist of points is provided for you.

The Parents as Educators Programme

This example concerns a programme set up in the city of Norwich in Norfolk through a local FE college. The name of the programme was stolen from a similar provision operated by the Open College of the North West. This particular project was developed in 2002 in response to the Learning and Skills Council's invitation for bids to run Local Initiative Funding Projects. The initial idea was to develop a programme for parents to help with their children's learning, particularly in the areas of science and mathematics. The primary aim was to support parents to support their children. The secondary aim was to help these young parents themselves gain confidence in learning, thereby encouraging them to progress to further mainstream course programmes.

Getting going

> Three out of four girls that went on the course (PaE) are not normally those that will participate in things, but were prepared to because of the way the Project Co-ordinator had built a relationship with them and the one we had with them allowed us to encourage them, so it was a case of different agencies working together . . . they liked the course . . . at least two of them have decided to go on and do other courses.
> (Response from partner organization to the programme, in Desira, 2003: 21).

To briefly explain the significant amount of work that goes into such developments is a difficult task, but any bid for funding from the local LSC was placed against national priorities and would normally result (as it did here) in something of a negotiation between the funder and the provider. Matters were further complicated by funding being available from different budgets. To qualify for one budget the programme needed to be verified by the Open College Network. This involved a considerable degree of preparation. To draw monies from the Local Initiative Fund, other aspects of the programme needed to be modified. The programme also qualified for other initiative budgets, but needed further adaptation. There is too little room here to go into precise details, but hopefully by this stage you can already appreciate the complexity (and frustration) involved in making such bids. However, the programme emerged for the following client group:

- Wards with the highest number of young people who had not obtained Level 2 qualifications were to be targeted.
- Students needed to be under 25 years of age.
- Students could not have previous L2 (or higher) qualifications.
- Ninety students was the target recruitment.
- Twenty students needed to complete CLAIT Plus at Level 2.

The original bid was proposed in September and rewritten in November, verified by the OCN in February and started properly in March with the appointment of a programme manager. It took six months of work to secure a £70,000 budget.

Points to think about

- The lead-in time from the initial idea to its realization was 6–7 months. Most FE colleges have a cyclical course approval deadline, which means that rapid responses are very difficult to achieve.
- What you set out to develop may not be the course that you had envisaged. You need to hit the funding criteria.
- Attracting external funding meant gaining the approval of the institution, the funding agency and the validating agency. Each has its own QA protocols and documentation.
- Course administration can be very heavy.
- Course approval and funding goes at the pace of the slowest and you cannot get going until everything is agreed.

What problems might these issues present to a course team in an FE setting?

The course design

[M]any of the group had had fractured schooling and the last thing I wanted to do was to put them off learning by throwing loads of ideas at them. I just wanted to get them use to thinking a little deeper and being confident enough to talk.

(Course tutor in Desira, 2003: 14)

The course was for young parents with children of primary school age and was comprised of three modules: Starting Science, Numbers for Children and CLAIT Plus. The first two were verified at Levels 1 and 2, the differentiation being based on assessment outcomes (for Level 1 a more straightforward assessment was required). The first two modules were based around Key Stage 1 of the National Curriculum (www.curriculumonline.gov.uk/) in science and maths. The students would carry out the kinds of activities that their children would do in class. The programme was to be a practical 'hands-on event' one morning a week for eight weeks, for each module. The sessions were to be informal, yet informative, fun to be part of and directly relevant beyond the classroom. The students had an additional debrief session to inform on the educational purpose of the activity. They were free discussions where the parents were encouraged to reflect and evaluate the activity. They were then encouraged to carry out the activity with their own children and to attempt to further evaluate its potential worth through practical application.

This evaluative feedback formed the first session of the following week's class. A new activity was then carried out and once again the parents were encouraged to evaluate it by carrying it out at home.

Points to think about

- User-friendly staff and those sympathetic to adult learners need to make up the team. Unfortunately, not all colleagues fall into these categories.
- The curriculum needs very obvious relevance.
- Cultural sensitivity, in its very widest sense, is vitally important.
- Inclusion in FE relates to delivery. Each session needs to be differentiated so as to include every learner.
- Be flexible – if something is not working, the team needs to be able to respond quickly and effectively.
- Are you (as the teacher) enjoying the sessions?
- Get students thinking about exits early.

Recruitment

[A] lot of people feel they have enough in their lives doing the basics, taking their children here and there, providing food. So people have to be quite motivated to even look for anything and then to go along every week.

(Student response, in Desira, 2003: 23)

Despite the preferences of college marketing units, practitioners generally regard blanket marketing as ineffective – it is expensive and rarely works. Within a time constraint of a project, collaboration with other organizations is one of the most important aspects to working with excluded groups. Contacting groups is the easy part however, what is more difficult is making collaboration productive. This requires openness and planning, as similar provision can sometimes be seen as competition between organizations. Such relationships also require parity of status – small community-based organizations are just as important, if not more so, than an FE college or a local university. Regular contact needs to be maintained and a shared commitment is needed to make things work. Lack of time is a very real pressure point here, in terms of both the project's life span and the time that staff from external organizations and team members can commit.

Some of the groups contacted through the PaE Project

- First schools
- Play groups, pre-school nurseries and toddler groups
- County Council Social Services, Probation Service, Community and Community Health Centres
- Organizations and networks supporting young adults
- Sure Start and Family First
- Community and Neighbourhood Centres
- Young parents such as Young Fathers and Embrace Young Mums
- Norfolk Family Learning Programme
- Adult Education Service
- Norwich City Council Community Services – Housing Services and Housing Associations
- Norfolk Traveller Education Service
- Community Breast Feeding Support Group
- Community Liaison (Norfolk Police)
- Early Years Network and Early Years Development Partnership
- Women's Refuge
- Advice Services.

With the Parents as Educators programme, the most successful recruitment strategy was through direct contact. A travelling science/maths activity workshop was developed known as 'Crash, Bang, Whallop' (OK, we were not very good with names!) and, working with local primary schools in the identified districts, toured around these schools putting on science fairs immediately after school hours. The hands-on nature of the activities ensured a very high attendance. This, in a rather underhand way, was something of a ruse, as although it was good for the children, it allowed other team members to approach waiting parents. This was the primary point of contact and was subsequently identified as the most effective marketing method (Desira, 2003). In this way, groups of young parents, who, even if not friends, were at least familiar with one another, were encouraged to take part. Getting groups of parents from these schools was one of the most effective recruitment tools for this project.

Probably the greatest pressure point with widening participation projects is actualizing recruitment. Difficult to reach groups are so called for a reason and sometimes, despite great amounts of work, potential clients do not enrol and targets are not met. The published literature will always concentrate, understandably, on successful projects but it can give the impression that everybody else is successful in recruiting these groups except you. In that context and with the pressure from funding agencies, managers (each with their own targets to meet) realizing that recruitment on a project is not strong can find the situation a significant source of stress. What is exceptionally important here, but difficult to achieve for some, is that there should be no fear of failure and no subsequent guilt. This later point is very important in cash-strapped adult education. After all, what is the worse that can happen? No one turns up – but you have tried – you will have really tried.

Unlocking the door

[R]eally it's justifying the time, if they have kids, they might have a part-time job and that can be really exhausting, because they're doing all sorts of things.
(Student response in Desira, 2003: 23).

For many adults there are no real reasons for not being able to return to education – there are very strong reasons why some cannot. Obstacles to returning are difficult to classify into groups, but there are a broad range of physical or mechanical restraints, such as finance (simply being able to afford it), childcare, travel, employment, home and care commitments. Each one of these needs to be considered carefully during programme development and the bid must include mechanisms to negate these obstacles.

Funds were used for the following

- Childcare for the duration of the course – by crèche or approved childminder.
- Transport costs to and from the centre.
- Fees – all fees were waived.
- Consumables.
- A day trip to a hands-on science exhibition.
- Minibus hire for trip.

Can you think of other uses of funds to encourage recruitment?

Another range of potential obstacles to returning to education may be social, or cultural. These are often recognized and discussed, but tend to be the issues that as practitioners we can do least about. Cultural pressures on any individual can be summarized as the degree by which the decision is seen as 'abnormal' by friends and relatives. Such reactions can be powerfully dissuasive, even to the extent of simply excluding further education as an option. Even to a lesser extent, negative comments at home, socially or in the workplace (even jocular ones along the lines of you are wasting your time) can become at best wearing, at worst self-fulfilling. Returning to learn can mark you out and as such lead to feelings of isolation. It is also a high-risk strategy. To study and to test oneself so openly and then to fail may result in some sort of confirmation of a sense of failure. Most commentators would suggest that confidence is the key to at least addressing some of these problems and one effective way around a sense of isolation or lack of confidence is to encourage and foster a close group atmosphere. It is one of the most well-worn truisms of FE to say that the single most important source of support for returning students is that given by other students.

Promoting confidence on the PaE Programme

- Do not teach at college, teach at school if accommodation is available.
- Empowerment of students – adult returners' last experience of education was school. They need to feel like adults. It sounds obvious, but it is vital to treat them as such. Their experience should be as far from a school environment as possible.

⇨

- It is important that the staff team engage with the students in an informal, non-intimidating way.
- Provide academic support. We also arranged talks from the adult guidance team.
- Be flexible in terms of delivery. One way is to not overfill the curriculum. Build in plenty of review time and tutorials. Respond to requests.
- Have fun in the sessions. We used trips out to break up the units.
- Place stress on personal goals and concentrate on positive feedback.

Can you think of other appropriate ways to build confidence?

The 'R' word – retention issues

[I]f my son had been happier in the crèche and it had been on the days I didn't have to work . . . I didn't want to give up, but at the same time thought what's the point? If there were different circumstances, I'd have seen it through.

(Student response in Desira, 2003: 34)

Probably the best advice for any new lecturer in adult education is to get used to discussing retention. Keeping students on a programme or a course is equally as hard as getting them on to the course in the first place.

The problem is a difficult one and it is compounded in the first instance quite simply by the fact that adults have complex lives. Childcare arrangements collapse, children fall ill, personal or social situations change. A young (particularly single) parent's life can suffer from variable and unforeseen pressures and when these mount up, it is understandable that the course is the first thing to suffer. Sometimes, particularly on higher level courses such as Access, it can be the case that a student will struggle with the workload and will increasingly feel overwhelmed, at which point all the original anxieties will return. Having a tangible 'problem' outside of college is, to a degree, a face-saving way of leaving the course without having failed. (Tony Brown in Chapter 3 offers a psycho-analytic interpretation for the kind of difficulty that learning situations can provoke, and how individuals choose to manage them.) The problem this presents to us as tutors is that as students leave for valid extraneous reasons, it may very well hide significant flaws in course design.

Unfortunately, retention will always be more likely to affect adult education and it is an issue that is difficult to address. Pre-course interviews are important in terms of pointing out to potential students some of the stresses that they may feel under, but, paradoxically, at the same time the interviewer is actively encouraging the student to enrol. In reality, the relationship between recruitment and retention is rarely the inverse; however, an interesting question to consider is how far do concerns about retention and completion rates act as yet another obstacle to participation?

There is a growing literature on improving retention rates (Thomas et al., 2003) and the topic is too complicated to discuss here, but certainly tutorial support, differentiated outcomes, individual learning plans, in fact all the components of good 'inclusive learning' help to retain students.

Maintaining retention

- No amount of information will ever be enough to replace experience – however, guidance interviews are essential.
- On-course tutorials (both academic and pastoral) – these can be quite informal.
- Act quickly on student feedback and comment.
- Flexible delivery (in the community, sympathetic timetables, measured curriculum).
- Flexibility and differentiation relating to assessments.

Can you think of others?

The end

The exit interviews formed the basis for feedback and intended follow-up sessions and throughout these interviews one constant theme emerged, namely that of an associated improvement in the student's personal confidence. Indeed, all students mentioned this. Some 89 per cent of the cohort, by the time of interview, intended to return to some form of full-time or part-time education. One aspect of offering such programmes is the academic parity that they have relative to other provision, particularly within the FE sector. To promote a sense of achievement and to raise the profile of the programme, at the end of each unit, there was a party and an official awards ceremony was arranged. The impact of such activities should never be underestimated. Think of how you will feel when you graduate.

Evaluating a programme

In June of 2003 the pilot programme had recruited thirty-five students yet the target had been seventy; meeting only half of the target figure was disappointing.

Of the thirty-five students, twenty-six completed the course, a 76 per cent completion rate, not too bad, but not great. In an earlier section of this chapter, dealing with disappointment was mentioned; certainly the course team thought this was a successful result, particularly given the conditions on recruitment laid down by the LSC: 'I can't think of anything else that we could have done, to contact or to encourage . . . I think [we] worked incredibly hard and did everything [we] could' (Project manager in Desira, 2003).

> ## Read the following
>
> It is because it is very difficult to reach client group. If you imagine having a baby when you are fourteen, really learning about Maths and Science is not top of your priority list is it? It is whether your housing is secure and a lot of them aren't in secure housing, even the ones that did make it on to the course. It was a very, very difficult client group to try to persuade back in.
>
> (Project coordinator in Desira, 2003).
>
> Do you think the PaE programme was appropriate for this client group? Would a more generic 'parenting' course have been more so?

Quantitative mechanisms are often used in the adult education sector, but this programme was also evaluated using qualitative methods in an attempt to explore the perceptions and experiences of a 'purposive' sample of the staff team and students (purposive sampling allows cases to be selected to illustrate particular features that may be of interest (Silverman, 2000: 104).

Course data were collected via semi-structured interviews with a selection of participants, to provide views on the project and how it had impacted on their aspirations for the future. Staff and the project manager were also interviewed; the cost of this independent survey had been built into the budget to help inform future projects.

Conclusions

It is difficult to draw conclusions on the relative success or failure of this programme. It missed its enrolment targets by quite a wide margin and nearly a quarter of the students did not complete. It involved a great deal of work from the team and like many such courses provided everyone, staff and students alike, with considerable levels of stress. Having said that, just spend some time to read through the following quotes taken from the course evaluation documentation (Desira, 2003): it may help you draw your own conclusions.

In relation to the course design and delivery

[W]ell there was a very diverse range of abilities, so there had to be a lot of differentiation. Obviously the more able students were doing it to support their children and out of interest as to what their children would be doing at School, whereas the less able students really needed support in becoming more confident in getting involved in the activities.

(Staff A in Desira, 2003: 15)

We walked down to the park and just chatted . . . it was good to just sit and talk about stuff. So yes, it was a good time.

(Student in Desira, 2003: 30)

It was quite interesting, it was funny, we had a laugh you know. It was quite relaxed . . . a lot of it was group work and we sort of chatted about it in groups rather than working alone and that was good, because we were all just discussing things freely.

(Student in Desira, 2003: 30)

It's quite good really, to know what the children are doing at school and you can actually help them at home . . . You can talk about things . . . It's changed my confidence in like, you know, helping the children learn and like that.

(Student in Desira, 2003: 31)

Conclusions on the Programme

It made me want to go to do bigger things now . . . it's got me back to College again and that's something I was really nervous about doing, so I think that's the biggest thing actually . . . it's got me back here and more confident.

(Student in Desira, 2003: 34)

I still feel during the week I got nothing to do. I mean, yeah, you can go out with friends and things when they're at school and that, but I just need more than that now . . . I just need to use my brain a bit more . . . as long as I get some sort of knowledge now and again, I'm happy.

(Student in Desira, 2003: 34)

Perhaps this shows you a different view when it comes to evaluating such programmes. To help you further, think of the course that you are on now. Is it inspirational? Is it promoting in you the desire for further study? Is it improving your confidence and increasing your interest in your own education? It is an important point to consider as this is precisely what widening participation in adult education and not necessarily training, based on these results, can seemingly provide.

One other point is that the Parents as Educators project eventually spent around half of its £70,000 budget. That's about £1,000 per student enrolled, for a Level 1 or Level 2 qualification. A valid question would be to ask if this level of funding is appropriate. Earlier in this chapter you were asked to reflect on your motivations for study, at this point it may be worthwhile briefly reflecting on the costs of your study, since the age of sixteen. Level 3 qualifications (such as A Level) are expensive to fund and any tuition fees paid at undergraduate level are only 'top up' fees, the substantial part is still centrally funded. It is equally valid to ask if this funding is appropriate. You are best placed to answer this.

To make a final point here, I again need to speak to you directly. Because of the annual funding cycle, Parents as Educators closed when the funding ended at the end of the academic year and as a result the networks and community links built up by the team also came to an end. It only ran for a short time but I often think back to it and those young parents who, despite all of the obstacles, still enrolled. I wonder now, nearly five years later, what has happened to them all? All I can hope is that they have maintained their confidence and their friendships.

A short adult education course such as this may not have radically changed their lives, but it changed mine. By being involved it somehow reaffirmed my commitment to widening participation in education. Yes, we went for a walk in the park, and yes, we had a laugh. Promoting the confidence to ask and to question, to develop a sense of real inclusion to the point where it is OK to laugh. To be comfortable with one another – and with oneself.

For me, these terribly ill-defined and elusive outcomes, which are so difficult to quantify, are crucially important prerequisites to the success of the wider aim of social inclusion. So, I am glad that, 'Yes, it was a good time', because, to really succeed, such courses have to be.

Author's note

> A poor year for Roger as his boisterous fooling has constantly undermined our good feelings towards him.

So concludes my final year report from school. Previous ones were littered with such comments as 'easily distracted' and 'must pay more attention'. With hindsight my problem was failing to cope with boredom and my impatience to leave was seemingly only matched by my school's wish to see the back of me. I am not at all bitter, I just did not get school and like a lot of people at 16 I had too much going on to worry about it.

Work helped me shake off the malaise and eventually I did start paying attention long enough to get back into learning. I ended up developing and managing one of the biggest Access programmes in the country, allowing thousands of adult students, failed by schools, to return to education. I have no philosophical conversion, nor intellectual construct to impart beyond my own experience that school is not everything and that we can learn at all stages of our lives.

References

Department for Education and Employment (DFEE) (1998), *The Learning Age: A Renaissance for a New Britain.* (Cm 3790). London: The Stationery Office.

Desira, C. (2003), *An Independent Evaluation of the LSC Funded Level 2 Local Initiative Fund Parents as Educators and CLAIT Plus Project. Final Report.* The Research Centre, Norwich City College.

Elsey, B. (1987), 'R.H. Tawney – Patron Saint of Adult Education', in P. Jarvis, *20th Century Thinkers in Adult Education.* London: Croom Helm.

FEFC (1996), *Inclusive Learning* (The Tomlinson Report). Coventry: FEFC/HMSO.

Field, J. (2006), *Lifelong Learning and the New Educational Order.* Stoke on Trent: Trentham Books.

Florian, L. (1998), 'Inclusive practice: What, why and how?', in C. Tilstone, L. Florian and R. Rose (eds), *Promoting Inclusive Practice.* London: Routledge.

Gibson, S. and Blandford, S. (2005), *Managing Special Educational Needs in Primary and Secondary Schools.* London: Sage.

HEFCE (2008), 'Growth in students on foundation degrees is on track to meet government target'. www.hefce.ac.uk/news/hefce/2008/founddeg.htm (accessed 10 July 2008).

Kelly, T. (1970), *A History of Adult Education in Great Britain.* Liverpool: Liverpool University Press.

Kennedy, H. (1997), *Learning Works – Widening Participation in Further Education.* FEFC: Coventry.

Learning and Skills Council (2007). www.lsc.gov.uk/Aboutus/ (accessed 10 July 2008).

Rosenthal, H. (2001), 'Discussion paper—working towards inclusion: "I am another other"', *Educational Psychology in Practice,* 17(4), 385–392.

Silverman, D. (2000), *Doing Qualitative Research*. London: Sage.

Summers, J. (2007), 'Kennedy revisited: we know how to widen participation, now we need to make it happen', in A. Tucket (ed.), *Participation and the Pursuit of Equality: Essays in Adult Learning, Widening Participation and Achievement*. Leicester: NIACE.

Tawney, R.H. (1950), *Social History and Literature* (7th National Book League Annual Lecture (1950), delivered 25th October 1959, Cambridge). Oxford: Oxford University Press.

Tawney, R.H. (1964), *Radical Tradition: Twelve Essays on Politics, Education and Literature*. Edited by Rita Hinden with a postscript by Hugh Gaitskell. New York: Pantheon Books.

Taylor, R. (2007), 'Social Class and Widening Participation', in A. Tucket (ed.), *Participation and the Pursuit of Equality*. Leicester: NIACE.

Thomas, L., Cooper, M. and Quinn, J. (eds), (2003) *Improving Completion Rates Among Disadvantaged Students*. Stoke-on-Trent: Trentham Books.

Tucket, A. (2008), 'Further falls', *Education Guardian*, 15 January. http: //education.guardian. co.uk/further/opinion/story/0,,2240690,00.html

Index

Note: Diagrams are given in *italics*.

Access programmes 152, 159, 164
adult education
    interest increases/funding
        reductions 152–3
    introduction 147–8
    PaE retention issues/evaluation 159–63
    Parents as Educators' programme
        (PaE) 153–60
    purpose 148–51
after-education (Freud) 57–9
annual reviews 16
anthroposophy 129
Armstrong, D. 17
attachment theory (Bowlby) 38, 51
authoritarianism 80
automaton conformity 80

Bachelard, G. 32
Baden-Powell, Baron Robert 124
Bailey, R. 125
Barnlee community 22–3
Bauman, H. D. L. 68
Baylis, Dr Nick 100
Berlin, I. 78
Bion, W. 60
Black pupils 13
Blair, Tony 151
Blunkett, David 150
Bohm, David 84–5
Bowlby, John 38, 51
Brin, Sergei 138
Britzman, D. 57
Brockwood Park School 84

Brookfield, S. 96
Brown, Tony 5, 47, 77, 110, 159
Bruner, Jerome 31, 47–8
Buddhism 95–6, 100
Burke, P. J. 72
Buxton, L. 53

Calvin, John 30
Cambridge University 99, 100
Cameron, David 98
Camphill Movement 129
case studies
    1 19
    2 20–3
    choosing to learn 83
    countryside college 129–30
    freedom and social change 84–5
    The Gables 127–8
Castells, M. 135
Centre for Supported Learning
        see Derby College for Deaf People
children
    active thinkers, learning through
        interaction 31
    children's courts idea 32
    encouragement for expressiveness/
        independence 34
    introduction 28
    as learners 29
    listening to 35–6
    mini-adult construct 30
    and the Mosaic approach 34
    opinions to be counted 40

children *Continued*
philosophy approach 38–9, 41, 85–8
  rights 32
  and UN Convention 33, 36
  and wellbeing 100
Christianity 21
Christie, E. 125
Clark, A. 35
Clark, Richard E. 139, 140
Clarke, Arthur C. 144
Clough, P. 108
Code of Practice, Special Educational Needs (DfES) 15–16
Cole, T. 109, 111
computer assisted learning (CAL) 139
Conrad Report 66–7
constructivist model 47
consultation 28, 34–6
consumerist approaches 52
counselling 61, 99
criticality 5, 75, 76, 85, 88
"Culture of Silence" (Freire) 14
Cutting, Roger 7, 55

Damascio, A. 54
Daniel, H. 111
Davies, B. 13, 14
Davis, L. J. 68
Day, C. 55
De Graaf, J. 97
deaf culture
  closure of residential schools 68–70
  deaf learners 66–8
  deafhood 65–6
  and higher education 70–2
  introduction 64–5
  learning with and from 72–3
  valuing 70
"Deaf President Now" movement 71
"democratic authority" 81
Derby College for Deaf People 71–2
Derrida, Jacques 68
Deschooling Society (Illich) 83–4, 89
Desforges, C. 122
destructive detachment 51–2
destructiveness 80
Dewey, J. 31
Dialogues (Plato) 29

disability 12, 14
Disability Discrimination Act (DDA) 136
Dismore, H. 125
Doddington, C. 87
Duke of Edinburgh Award Scheme 121, 124

'E' is for Everything, The (Katz/ Oblinger) 136–7
e-learning
  conclusions 144
  digital divides 136
  enhanced learning 141–2
  everywhere 142–3
  exclusion 143
  extended learning 140–1
  introduction 134–5
  learners 139–40
  nature 138–9
  pervasive, ubiquitous/ indispensable 137–8
East Anglia University 39, 41
Ecclestone, K. 99
Education Act 1981 12
Elton Report 1989 (DfES) 109
emotions 49–50, 53–5, 60–1, 100
European Council 135
Evans, J. 15
Every Child Matters 2003 (DfES) 27, 114
experiential learning cycle 127
experimental schools 82

Faith and Light (2007) 20–1
Farrell, P. 113
Fear of Freedom, The (Fromm) 77–8, 89
Fernandes, Jane 71
forest schools 121, 123
Frederickson, N. 105–7
free schools 82
freedom
  and alternative schools 82–5
  and educational philosophy 80–2, 88–9
  interpretations of 77–9
  introduction 76
  and mainstream education 85
  negative/positive 78–9, 86–7
Freire, Paulo 3, 14, 76, 80–1
Freud, Sigmund 57

Friendship and Caring Trust
(FACT) 21–3
Friquegnon, Marie-Louise 31
Froebel, Friedrich 29
Fromm, E. 76–80, 88–9
Furedi, Frank 98–9
Further Education Funding Council
(FEFC) 152

Gallaudet University, Washington,
DC. 70–1
Gallions Primary School 39, 86–8
Gibson, Suanne 2, 4, 17, 126, 151
Giroux, Henry 3, 54
Goodley, D. 91
Grace, G. 18–19

Hahn, Kurt 124
Haidt, J. 95
happiness 6, 92–5, 98, 101
Harris, B. 105
Harvard University 99
Harvey, Jeremy 15
Hayes, D. 128
Hayes, J. 16
Haynes, Joanna 4–6, 94, 95, 136
Head, G. 110
"hedonic treadmill" (Haidt) 95
Hitzhusen, G. 124
Holt, J. 84
Honore, C. 100–1
human rights 27, 32–5
Human Scale Education 82
Hutchison, Alan 5, 82

Illich, Ivan 83–4, 89
In Praise of Slow (Honore) 100–1
*Inclusion: Does it Matter Where Pupils are
Taught?* 2006 (Ofsted) 116
Inclusive Learning see Tomlinson Report
(FEFC, 1996)
income/happiness diagram *94*
India 101–2
informal learning
benefits of outdoors 125
best practice 128–9
introduction 121–2
nature 122–3

outdoor opportunities *123*
outdoors 122–7
and schooling *122*
information and communication
technologies (ICTs) 135, 140, 144
Internet 7, 134–5, 137–9

Jacobs, J. A. 124–5
James, A. 35
James, O. 97
Jonassen, D. H. 139, 140
Jones, J. E. 127
Judith (example) 56

Katz, Richard 136–7, 144
Kelly, G. A. 54
Kelly, P. 122
Kelly, T. 148
Kennedy Report (Kennedy 1997) 150–1
Key Stage 1, National Curriculum 155
Knowler, Helen 6, 54, 98
Kolb, D. A. 127
model (1984) 127
Korczak, Janusz 32–3
Kozma, R. B. 139
Krishnamurti, Jidhu 76, 84–5, 88
Kumar, Satish 102

Ladd, P. 66, 69
Layard, R. 93–5, 97, 101
league tables 3, 15, 18, 106, 109
"learned failure" (Holt) 84
*Learning Age,
The* 1998 (Green Paper) 150–1
Learning and Skills Act (2000) 152
Learning and Skills Council (LSC) 152–3
Learning Works see Kennedy Report
(Kennedy 1997)
Lewis, A. 17
"lifelong learning" 93
Lines, D. 110
Lipman, Matthew 41, 88
listening 4, 17, 28, 32,
34–8, 40, 42, 86, 88
Liverpool 82
Local Initiative Fund Projects
(LIF) 152–4
Locke, John 29

Loynes, C. 124
Lunt, I. 15

MacConville, R. 13–14, 19
McKenzie, M. D. 125
Manifesto for Outdoor Learning 126–7
Marx, Karl 78–9
Midlands Psychology Group 98–9
Mill, John Stuart 78
Mindfulness Education programme
    (Vancouver) 100
Mittler, P. 12
Morris, Ian 100
Mortimer, H. 16
Mortlock, C. 124
Mosaic approach 34
Murris, Karin 41

National Curriculum 110, 115, 128
Neill, A. S. 76, 83, 85, 88
neo-liberalism
    and contemporary education policy
      3, 14
    contradictions 15
    as dominant ideology 11
    and freedom 78
    impact on students 54
    knowledge as capital to invest 18
    pejorative ideology 13
    and teacher training 57
    turning back the tide 12, 17
Newton, J. 92
Nimier, J. 48
Noddings, Nel 2, 93, 94
Nundy, S. 125
nurture groups 37–8

Oaklee Housing Association 21
Oblinger, Diana 136–7, 144
O'Brien, T. 108, 110
Ofsted 18, 19, 39, 116
On Dialogue (Bohm) 84–5
On Liberty (Mill) 78
Open College Network 153

P4C (philosophy with children) 41
Parents as Educators' programme
    (PaE) 153–63

participation 35, 77, 93–4
Penn Resilience Project 100
personal constructs (Kelly) 54–5
Pestalozzi, Johann Heinrich 29
Pfeiffer, J. W. 127
phenomenology 32
Pirrie, A. 110
Plato 29
Polat, F. 113
Positive Psychology course (Tal Ben-
    Shahar) 99
"positive psychology" (Seligman et al) 96
Powers, S. 69
Prout, A. 35
psychoanalytic theory 47–9, 52–3
Pupil Referral Units (PRUs) 107
Putnam, R. 96

Quicke, J. 16

Rashid (example) 50
Rea, Tony 7
Reed, J. 114
reflexivity 16, 53
*Removing Barriers to
    Achievement* 2004 (DfES) 110
Ricketts, M. 127
Rickinson, M. 123, 125
Rogers, C. 111
Rosenthal, H. 11–12, 19
Rousseau, Jean-Jacques 29–30

Sacks, Oliver 64
Sally (example) 58–9
SAPERE (charity) 41
Sapon-Shevin, M. 14–15
Sasha (example) 49
school councils 39–40
school effectiveness 18, 106
Scout Movement, The 124
SEAL (Social and Emotional Aspects of
    Learning) project (DfES) 101
Seema (example) 50–1
Seligman, Professor Martin 100
Shepherd, I. 128
sign language 64, 66, 68–9, 73
Skelton, T. 67–70
Skills Plus 152

slow movement 100–1
Smith, Hannah 5, 107
Social and Emotional Aspects of
	Learning 2005 (SEAL) (DfES) 110
"social capital" (Putnam) 96
Social Emotional Behavioural Difficulties
	(SEBD)
	belonging 106–7, 113
	the burden 108–11
	introduction 104–6
	school placement 111–12, *113*, 114–16
social trust 96–7
Socrates 29, 38
Solomon, Y. 111
Special Education Needs (SEN) 16, 19,
	105, 108, 110, 115
Special Educational Needs and Disability
	Act (SENDA) 136
Stables, A. 122
Stanford University 138
Steiner, Rudolf 129
students
	and attachment theory 51
	conceptions of 51–2
	emotional context of learning 53–5
	identity disturbance 56–9
	learning spaces 59–60
	relationships to troublesome
		knowledge 48–9
	student-tutor relationships 53, 60–1
subject-subject relations 59
Summerhill educational community 83

Tawney, R. H. 148–9
Taylor, Tim 40
Ten Tors Challenge 126
Thinking Allowed
	(Gallions Primary School) 87
Tomlinson Report (FEFC 1996) 150–1
Train to Gain 152
Training and Enterprise Councils
	(TECs) 152

Tuckswood Community First School 36–40

U.N. Convention on Rights of the Child
	(1989) 27, 33, 36
unhappiness 97–8
UNICEF 36
United States *94*
"Unity for Gallaudet Now" 71

Valentine, G. 67–70
Verkuyten, M. 106
virtual learning environments
	(VLE's) 137–8
Visser, J. 107, 113
Vygotsky, Lev 31

Watts, M. 72
websites
	www.brockwood.org.uk 84
	www.cambridgewellbeing.org 100
	www.channel4.com 124
	www.creative-corner.co.uk 36, 38, 40
	www.curriculumonline.gov.uk 155
	www.dfee.gov 27
	www.hse.org.uk 82
	www.lifelonglearning.co.uk 150
	www.ofsted.gov.uk 37, 39
	www.sapere.org 41
	www.summerhillschool.co.uk 83
wellbeing
	conclusions 101
	education 92–7
	introduction 91–2
	politics of a wellbeing curriculum 98–101
Wellington College 100
Weyl-Kailey, L. 48
Wheeler, Steve 7
Willis, J. 127
Winnicott, D. W. 32, 59
Workers Educational Association
	(WEA) 148
Wrigley, O. 64